HOME REPAIR AND IMPROVEMENT

THE HOME WORKSHOP

TIME®
LIFE
BOOKS

OTHER PUBLICATIONS:

DO IT YOURSELF
The Time-Life Complete Gardener
Home Repair and Improvement
The Art of Woodworking
Fix It Yourself

COOKING
Weight Watchers® Smart Choice Recipe Collection
Great Taste/Low Fat
Williams-Sonoma Kitchen Library

HISTORY
The American Story
Voices of the Civil War
The American Indians
Lost Civilizations
Mysteries of the Unknown
Time Frame
The Civil War
Cultural Atlas

TIME-LIFE KIDS
Family Time Bible Stories
Library of First Questions and Answers
A Child's First Library of Learning
I Love Math
Nature Company Discoveries
Understanding Science & Nature

SCIENCE/NATURE
Voyage Through the Universe

For information on and a full description
of any of the Time-Life Books series listed above,
please call 1-800-621-7026 or write:

Reader Information
Time-Life Customer Service
P.O. Box C-32068
Richmond Virginia 23261-2068

THE HOME WORKSHOP

BY THE EDITORS OF TIME-LIFE BOOKS, ALEXANDRIA, VIRGINIA

The Consultants

Bruce M. Cuney has been a journeyman painter since 1971, and he began industrial painting for the California Institute of Technology's Palomar Observatory in 1978. His work there requires special knowledge of industrial finishes and rigging.

Richard Day, who has been writing in the home workshop field for 40 years, was a Home and Shop consulting editor for *Popular Science* magazine. A director and past-president of the National Association of Home and Workshop Writers, Mr. Day has also filled three self-built houses with furniture crafted in his workshop.

Giles Miller-Mead taught advanced cabinet-making at Montreal technical schools for more than 10 years. A native of New Zealand, he also served as a consultant on Time-Life's *The Art of Woodworking* book series, and constructed two houses of his own and several workshops.

Joe Teets is a master electrician/contractor with 20 years of experience. He has been involved in apprenticeship training as an instructor and coordinator since 1985, and is currently working in the Office of Adult and Community Education for Fairfax County Public Schools.

CONTENTS

Selecting and Adapting a Space

The ideal home workshop is a safe, efficient, and comfortable place to undertake projects ranging from cabinetmaking to repairing appliances. Once you have chosen your shop's location, you may need to modify the space, adding features like ventilation and soundproofing; bringing heat to the room; or improving access.

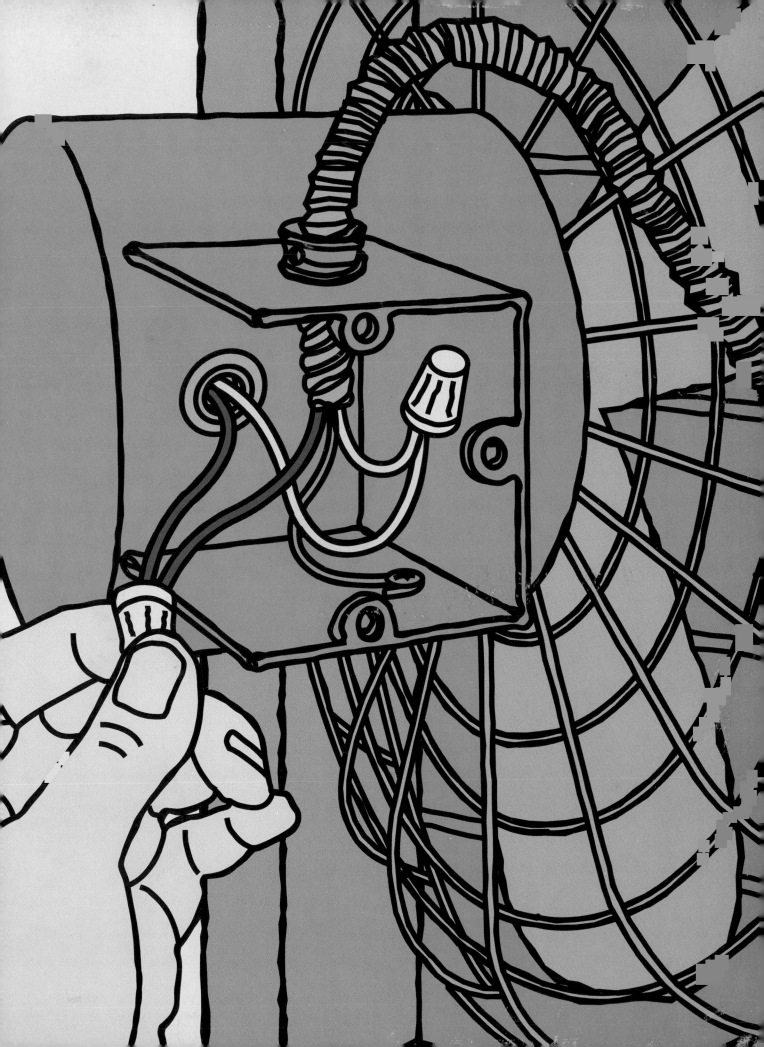

Home workshops are often improvised out of an area initially designed for some other purpose. This arrangement usually calls for some modifications, but with imagination and careful planning, you can create a workshop in almost any space.

Requirements: Features common to all well-designed shops include easy access; sufficient space for the chosen activity; and adequate electrical power, lighting, heat, and ventilation. Other factors such as soundproofing and storage space are important for some. Ponder the questions below and opposite to select a location, keeping in mind that you can add many features.

A Basement Shop: This location has several advantages over other rooms. It usually contains the furnace, so it is already heated; and it is generally isolated from the rest of the house, making it easier to contain dust and dirt. Its masonry foundation walls tend to block sound naturally, and the concrete floors found in most basements provide a sturdy foundation for heavy power tools.

A basement workshop may have drawbacks, however. The space may be moist, although dampness can sometimes be cured by improving drainage around the house and waterproofing the walls *(pages 12-13)*. In some basements, access may be limited, especially if the only entrance is through an inside door. Building an outside entrance can be a difficult or even impossible undertaking.

The Spare Room: One of the benefits of locating a shop in an unused room is that heating and electricity are readily available, and windows can provide light and ventilation. In many cases, however, the dust, dirt, and noise may disrupt others. Thorough soundproofing can reduce the noise level, and installing a door to the outside will keep dirt from being tracked into the house.

Upstairs: An attic can be ideal for small-scale activities like carving, model making, and other hobbies. Frequent trips to the attic with tools and materials can become a nuisance, however, and unless the ceiling is adequately insulated, the space may be too hot in summer or too cold in winter. If you use heavy machines, you may have to reinforce the floor to meet code requirements.

Sharing the Garage: Like a basement, a garage is generally isolated from the rest of the house, making it suitable for automotive work and other noisy or messy jobs. The wide door provides excellent access to the outside, and overhead storage room is often available under the rafters. In a long, narrow garage, you may be able to fit the work area at the back; if you place it on a side wall, leave 3 to 4 feet of clearance for opening car doors.

SEVEN IMPORTANT CONSIDERATIONS

What kind of work will you do?
Hobbies such as carving, model building, or jewelry making require relatively little space and can be done almost anywhere in the house. If you plan to build furniture or undertake other cabinetry projects, you will need room to accommodate stationary power tools *(pages 30-39)*, as well as for assembling and applying finishes to the projects.

How accessible is the site?
It is difficult to carry heavy machinery, unwieldy building materials, and finished projects into and out of a workshop through narrow doorways or up long flights of stairs. The ideal access is provided by double doors opening directly to the outside, with a minimum of steps to ground level, eliminating the problem of carrying cumbersome objects around corners, and cutting down on dirt tracked through the house. In some cases, you can add a pass-through *(pages 19-20)*.

What utilities are available?

All workshops need heat, light, and power, and many also need air conditioning or a water supply. If you choose a site inside the house, most utilities will be available, although you may have to tap into electrical circuits or extend the plumbing, heating, or cooling system. If you select a site that is detached from the house, it may be more difficult to provide utilities.

How much noise will you make?

Large power tools are noisy, and their vibrations may be carried through the house. You may have to install soundproofing—especially if you plan to use these tools late at night when people are asleep.

What are the storage possibilities?

In addition to work space, a workshop needs plenty of room to stow tools, hardware, and materials *(pages 106-121)*. The site you choose will need enough wall or ceiling space to contain shelves, cabinets, and storage racks. Keep in mind that exposed ceiling joists or wall studs can be adapted for adding such storage facilities.

Can you control moisture and ventilation?

Excessive dampness is a menace in a workshop: It can rust tools, warp wood, and mar newly applied finishes such as paint and varnish. Locating a shop above ground level reduces the risk of dampness; in a basement you may have to install a dehumidifier. Poor ventilation can make a shop unbearably stuffy, and even dangerous when toxic and flammable fumes are present. The more windows the room has, the better.

What will you do with dirt and dust?

Dirt and dust are inevitable by-products of workshop activity. An efficient cleaning system will control most of the mess *(pages 122-125)*, but the closer the shop is to living quarters, the harder it will be to keep dust out of other areas.

SHOPS IN UNEXPECTED PLACES

If there is no obvious location for a workshop in your house or garage, there may still be a suitable space that you have overlooked. You can tuck a small work area under a basement stairway or in a closet *(page 47)*. In the laundry room, you can build a hinged worktable that folds down over the washer and dryer, and install shelves above for storage. Another option is to locate a shop in an enclosed porch. In a region with a warm climate, you may be able to adapt an open porch, or even a concrete patio sheltered by a sunroof. With this arrangement, mount wheels on the bench and heavy tools so they can be rolled inside for storage. If your yard is large enough and building codes permit it, you can erect a utility shed.

Building In Safety Features

Wearing the appropriate safety gear for the job and practicing safe work habits will prevent many injuries, but you can help ensure your safety by building it right into the shop.

Ease of Access: Making it easy to move materials is one way to eliminate accidents. Design doorways at least 36 inches wide. If you have space for them, mount double doors 72 inches wide.

Codes generally require that stairways have treads at least 10 inches wide and risers no more than $8\frac{1}{4}$ inches high. Apply nonskid tape or corrugated rubber pads to the treads and paint the nosings—the front edges of the treads—yellow. Attach a sturdy handrail along one side.

Make sure the shop floor is durable, skidproof, and easy to clean. Keep it free of obstructions. If you install an electrical raceway to a floor outlet, paint it with black and yellow stripes so it is clearly visible.

Electrical Safety: Your workshop will need a safe and adequate supply of electricity *(pages 48-61)*. To prevent unauthorized use of power tools, consider installing a lockable service panel and switch plates, or disabling the plugs of power tools *(opposite)*. To meet your lighting requirements *(pages 62-67)*, supplement natural light from windows with overhead fluorescent fixtures, and install clamp-on desk lights for localized lighting. Shield all lamps with metal mesh.

Invisible Hazards: Although seemingly innocuous by-products of shop activity, dust and noise pose a serious health threat. Proper shop ventilation is essential *(pages 17-18)*. Wherever possible, sheathe the shop with materials that muffle sound and mount power tools on rubber pads *(page 21)*. Minimize the disturbance to others with soundproofing *(pages 22-23)*.

Safe Storage: Place racks and shelves so they are accessible but out of the way. Lock up potentially dangerous tools, and store flammable liquids in locked metal cabinets. Dispose of debris in metal trash cans with lids, and empty them frequently.

Keep a first-aid kit in a handy location. Stock it with basic supplies such as gauze, tape, scissors, bandages, disinfectant, antiseptic cream, tweezers, and an eye-wash solution—and check it frequently to restock depleted items.

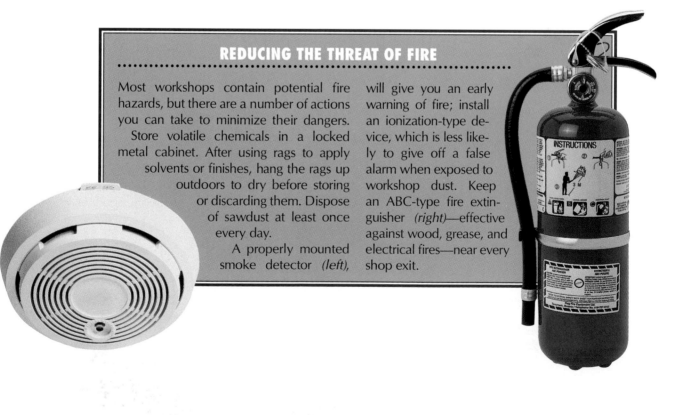

REDUCING THE THREAT OF FIRE

Most workshops contain potential fire hazards, but there are a number of actions you can take to minimize their dangers.

Store volatile chemicals in a locked metal cabinet. After using rags to apply solvents or finishes, hang the rags up outdoors to dry before storing or discarding them. Dispose of sawdust at least once every day.

A properly mounted smoke detector *(left)*, will give you an early warning of fire; install an ionization-type device, which is less likely to give off a false alarm when exposed to workshop dust. Keep an ABC-type fire extinguisher *(right)*—effective against wood, grease, and electrical fires—near every shop exit.

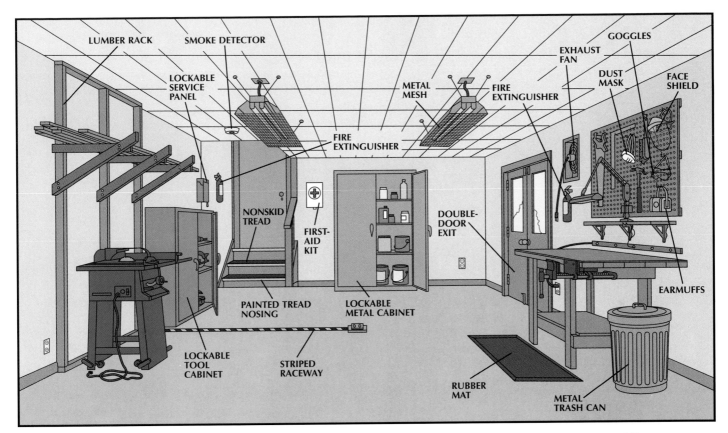

Designing a workshop for safety.

This workshop incorporates many of the safety features described opposite. In addition, the walls are sheathed with fire-retardant wallboard covered with fire-resistant latex paint in a light shade to brighten the shop and improve visibility. On the ceiling, acoustic tiles dampen noise levels.

Electrical power is available at outlets in many different areas, eliminating the need for extension cords. At the workbench, a rubber mat helps mitigate the fatigue that can result from standing on a concrete floor for long periods. Safety goggles, a face shield, and respiratory and hearing protectors are within easy reach.

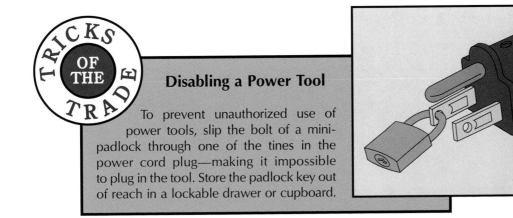

TRICKS OF THE TRADE

Disabling a Power Tool

To prevent unauthorized use of power tools, slip the bolt of a mini-padlock through one of the tines in the power cord plug—making it impossible to plug in the tool. Store the padlock key out of reach in a lockable drawer or cupboard.

Keeping a Basement Workshop Dry

Excess moisture is often a concern in a basement home workshop. Besides making a room uncomfortable, dampness can rust tools and warp wood.

Tracking the Moisture: To discover the source of the dampness, fasten a piece of foil 1 foot square to the inside of the basement wall, sealing all four edges with tape. After two days, check the foil. If moisture formed on the room side of the foil, the cause is condensation inside the room. If it appears on the side facing the wall, seepage from outside is the culprit. If both sides of the foil are wet, you have both problems.

Dealing with Condensation: Set up a dehumidifier; and in summer, use a window air conditioner to help keep the basement dry and cool. To control condensation dripping from cold-water pipes, cover them with foam pipe insulation.

Handling Seepage: If there is standing water near the foundation after a heavy rain, you may be able to solve the problem by repairing gutters or installing new ones. Also, check the walls for cracks. Although small fissures do not endanger the structure of a house, they can let water in—it's best to seal them. Horizontal cracks along a bulging wall or vertical cracks wider than $\frac{1}{4}$ inch and longer than 4 feet indicate a serious structural problem. If water is seeping through the joint between the basement floor and wall, the basement may lie below the water table. In either case, consult a building professional.

Sometimes, the only way to deal with a wet basement is to excavate along the outside of the foundation wall and add drain tile at the footing. The enormity of this job persuades most people to leave the work to a professional.

 TOOLS

Tape measure
Shovel
Caulking gun
Ball-peen hammer
Cold chisel
Stiff-fiber brush
Pointing trowel

 **MATERIALS**

Silicone caulk
Splash block
Latex concrete-
   patching compound
Plastic sheeting
Duct tape

SAFETY TIPS

Protect your eyes with goggles when chipping out masonry or mixing patching compound.

 **A HUMIDITY TESTER**

Available at a scientific-supply or electronic hobby store, a portable hygrometer is a simple way to measure relative humidity. Take a reading when the temperature in the basement is at its coolest, usually in the morning. If the humidity is above 70 percent, take steps to reduce it, as described above.

Locating the leaks.

◆ If pools of water collect near the house foundation, inspect the gutters. Clean them of debris and check that they slope toward a downspout by $\frac{1}{4}$ inch for every 20 feet of length. Arrange downspouts to direct water at least 3 feet away from the walls: Replace damaged splash blocks or add downspout extensions to direct water out into the yard.

◆ Bank soil away from the foundation and plant ground cover to hold the soil in place.

◆ Check basement window frames for leaks and seal any gaps with caulk; clear window wells of leaves that may block drainage and channel water into the basement.

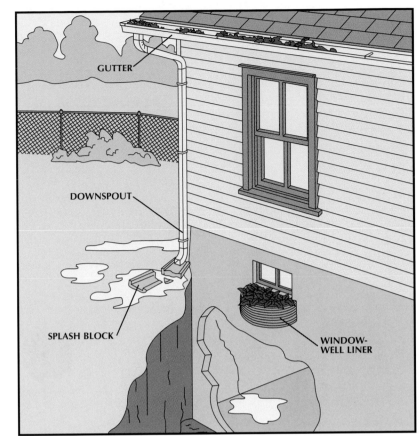

GUTTER

DOWNSPOUT

SPLASH BLOCK

WINDOW-WELL LINER

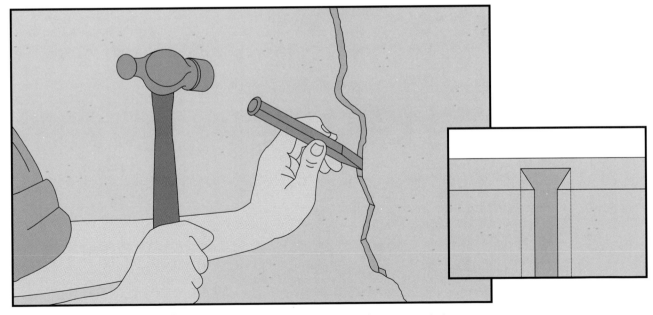

Patching small wall cracks.

With a cold chisel and a ball-peen hammer, enlarge the crack to about $\frac{1}{4}$ inch wide and $\frac{1}{2}$ inch deep (above), undercutting the opening (inset). If undercutting is impossible, make the sides straight rather than V-shaped.

◆ Clean out the crack with a stiff-fiber brush.

◆ Wet the crack or brush on a bonding agent, if necessary, then use a pointing trowel to fill the gap with latex concrete-patching compound.

◆ Starting at the top of the crack, pull the edge of the trowel down to remove excess compound.

◆ Smooth the patch with the back of the trowel.

◆ Tape plastic sheeting over the patch and let it cure.

When planning a heating scheme for a workshop, you'll need to isolate the heat source from any combustibles—especially if the heater uses exposed electric coils or an open flame.

Forced-Air Systems: Extending an existing forced-air system to a shop is the safest option. It is often the least expensive solution as well, requiring only that you run ductwork from the furnace to the shop. However, if the workshop is more than 25 feet from the furnace, or you cannot run the duct in a relatively straight line, most of the heat will dissipate before reaching the shop.

Electric Heat: An electric baseboard heater is a simple, if expensive, solution. These units fit against the wall, taking up little space. Some have a built-in thermostat; others are wired to a wall-mounted thermostat. The best arrangement is to install a 20-amp branch circuit from the service panel *(pages 54-57)* for a 240 volt-heater; a plug-in 120-volt model can overload the circuit serving it. To estimate the wattage you need, multiply the number of square feet in the shop by 10.

 TOOLS

Electric drill
Ball-peen hammer
Cold chisel
Tin snips
Screwdriver
Hammer
Electronic stud
  sensor
Wire stripper
Cable ripper

 **MATERIALS**

Starter collar
Round duct (6")
Sheet-metal screws
  ($\frac{1}{2}$" No. 10)
Furnace tape
Perforated metal
  strapping
Stove bolts, washers,
  and nuts
Joist-hanger nails
Register and boot
Screw anchors
Wood screws
  ($\frac{3}{4}$" No. 8)
2-wire grounded
  cable (No. 12)
Conduit
Cable staples
Cable clamp
Wire clamps

 **SAFETY TIPS**

Protect your eyes with goggles when chiseling, drilling, or nailing, and wear work gloves when handling sheet metal.

TAPPING INTO A FORCED-AIR FURNACE

1. Cutting into the main duct.
◆ With a felt-tipped pen, outline a 6-inch sheet-metal starter collar on the main duct, or plenum, at the top of the furnace. Drill a hole within the outline.
◆ With a hammer and a cold chisel, enlarge the hole enough to accommodate tin snips *(right)*.
◆ Cut the outline with the snips.

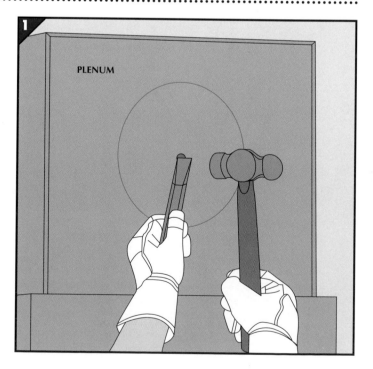

PLENUM

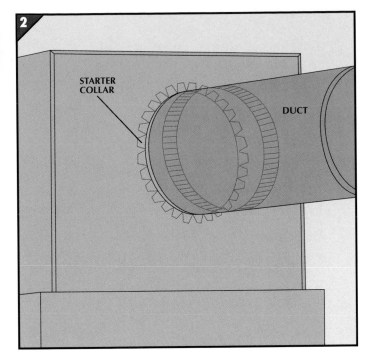

2. Securing the collar.

◆ Slide the starter collar, tabbed end first, into the opening so the bead encircling the collar sits against the plenum.

◆ Reach inside and fold the tabs against the plenum.

◆ Slide a section of round duct 6 inches long over the collar *(left)*.

◆ Drill a $\frac{1}{8}$-inch hole through each side of the joint, drive $\frac{1}{2}$-inch No. 10 sheet-metal screws into the holes, and seal the joint with furnace tape.

3. Supporting the duct.

◆ Screw on additional sections of duct. Every 3 feet, wrap a piece of perforated metal strapping around the duct and secure the strap to the duct with a stove bolt, washer, and nut.

◆ With a joist-hanger nail, fasten the strapping to a joist so there is at least 1 inch of clearance between the duct and the joist *(right)*.

◆ Wrap furnace tape around the joint.

If the joists are not exposed, locate them with a stud sensor and fasten the strapping to the bottoms of the joists through the ceiling material.

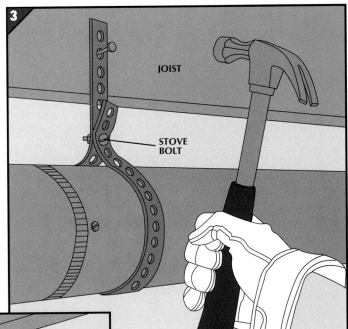

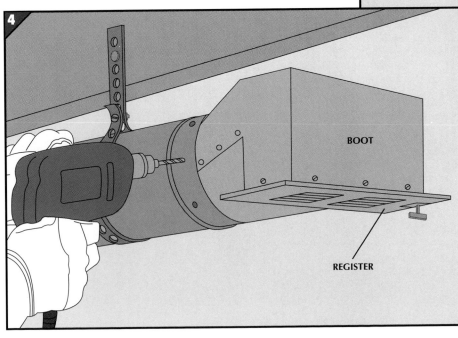

4. Assembling the register.

◆ Attach a register to the rectangular opening of a register boot by drilling matching screw holes through the flanges of the register and boot and fastening the two together with sheet-metal screws.

◆ Slide the boot over the end of the last section of duct. Drill holes through both *(left)* and screw them together.

◆ Wrap furnace tape around the joint.

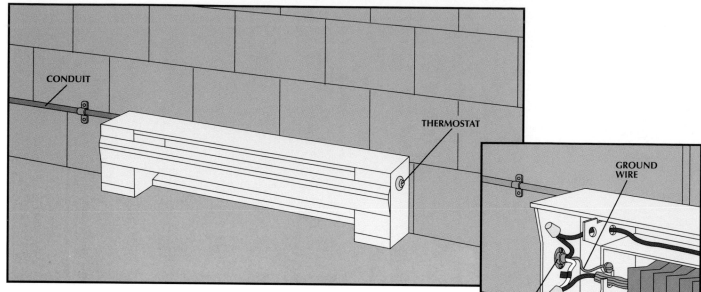

Wiring the heater.

◆ For a masonry wall, hold the heater against the wall and mark the positions of its mounting screws or clips; then drill holes at the marks and insert screw anchors. For a finished wall, remove the baseboard, then locate and mark the studs.

◆ Secure the heater to the masonry wall with the anchors, or to the studs with $\frac{3}{4}$-inch No. 8 wood screws.

◆ Run a length of 12-gauge electrical cable with conduit *(pages 54-55)* between the service panel and the heater, but do not connect the wiring.

◆ Run the cable to the heater's knockout hole and fasten it with a cable clamp, then strip about $\frac{3}{4}$ inch of insulation from the black and white wires.

◆ With wire caps, connect the black cable wire to a black heater wire; connect the white cable wire to the other black heater wire and wrap a piece of electrical tape around the white wire to recode it. Connect the bare cable ground wire to the grounding screw of the heater *(inset)*.

◆ Have an electrician connect the cable to the service panel.

A Warm Box for Cold Climates

To protect items like paint and finishes from freezing in a workshop detached from your house, you don't need to heat the entire shop around the clock. Instead, keep the items in a small cabinet and warm it with a low-surface-temperature "pump-house" heater. If the temperature in your shop will drop below 0°F, insulate the cabinet.

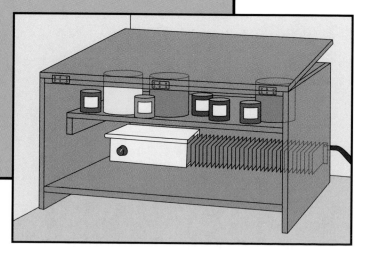

Adding an Exhaust Fan

Open windows and doors may provide enough air to dispel workshop fumes and airborne dust in good weather. For an all-weather solution, install a fan that vents directly outside through a wall opening or a hole in plywood set in a window.

Selecting a Fan: A regular kitchen fan that moves 425 cubic feet of air per minute is adequate for a workshop up to 1,700 cubic feet in size. Larger fans can be ordered. Divide your shop's cubic footage by four—the number of minutes in which the fan is required to completely change the air—to determine the size you need in cubic feet per minute (CFM).

If you will be cutting through a stud wall to accommodate a fan, select one that fits between two studs. Some fans have mounting holes 16 inches apart for attaching directly to adjoining studs; others require a frame for the fan housing *(page 18)*. A fan with an enclosed motor eliminates the danger of sparks that could ignite flammable or explosive fumes. A model with an automatic damper or shutters will keep out cold air.

If you plan to use a paint sprayer in the shop, you will need a more elaborate setup *(pages 100-102)*.

Dust Filters: Ambient air cleaners consist of a blower and a series of filters. They are ideal for removing dust from shop air; however, they cannot remove chemical fumes.

 TOOLS

Electronic stud
  sensor
Carpenter's level
Electric drill

Compass saw
Circular saw
Hammer
Caulking gun
Wire stripper
Cable ripper

 **MATERIALS**

Lumber ($\frac{3}{4}$" thick)
Common nails ($2\frac{1}{2}$")
Wood screws
  ($1\frac{1}{4}$" No. 8)

Silicone caulk
Armored electrical
  cable
Cable clamp
Wire caps

 **SAFETY TIPS**

Goggles protect your eyes when you are nailing or operating a power tool.

⚠ CAUTION

Asbestos and Lead

Before 1978, lead was used exclusively in paint, while asbestos was found in wallboard, joint compound, and insulation. Before cutting into walls or ceilings, mist the area with a solution of 1 teaspoon of low-sudsing detergent per quart of water, then cut out a small sample with a hand tool. Use a home test kit to check for lead; take asbestos samples to a certified lab. If either substance is present, you may want to hire a professional for the job; if you do the work yourself, follow these procedures:

❗ *Keep people and pets out of the work area.*

❗ *Wear protective clothing (available from a safety-equipment store) and a dual-cartridge respirator with high-efficiency particulate air (HEPA) filters. Remove the clothing before leaving the work area, wash it separately, and shower immediately.*

❗ *Indoors, seal off work-area openings, including windows, doors, vents, and air conditioners, with 6-mil polyethylene sheeting and duct tape. Cover nonremovable items with sheeting and tape, and turn off forced-air systems. Mop the area twice when the job is done. Outdoors, never work in windy conditions, and cover nearby ground with plastic sheeting.*

❗ *Never sand materials or cut them with power tools—mist them with detergent and remove them with a hand tool.*

❗ *Place all debris in a 6-mil polyethylene bag and call your health department or environmental protection agency for disposal guidelines.*

1. Cutting the inside opening.

◆ Locate the studs and mark their positions on the wall.

◆ Between two adjoining studs, outline the rough opening for the fan, using a level to keep the lines horizontal *(right)*.

◆ Turn off electrical power to the work area in case you cut into wires.

◆ Drill a hole through the wall at each corner of the outline. With a compass saw or saber saw, cut through the inside wall along the outline. Remove the wallboard and insulation.

◆ Working outside, cut a matching opening through the exterior wall, using the corner holes as reference points *(inset)*.

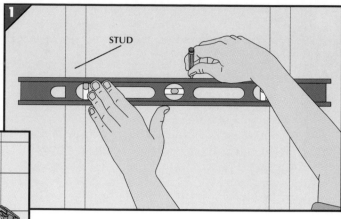

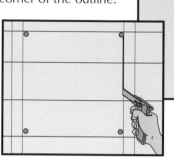

2. Inserting the frame.

◆ Measure the distance from the exterior to the interior wall surfaces, and cut a $\frac{3}{4}$-inch-thick board to your measurement.

◆ Cut the board into pieces to make a frame that fits exactly within the opening; assemble the frame with $2\frac{1}{2}$-inch common nails.

◆ Slip the frame into the opening *(left)* so the outside edge is flush with the sheathing, then nail it to the studs.

◆ Outside, mark the screw holes in the fan mounting flange on the edges of the frame and drill a $\frac{1}{8}$-inch pilot hole at each mark. Spread silicone caulk along the frame edges, set the fan in the frame, and secure it with $1\frac{1}{4}$-inch No. 8 wood screws *(inset)*.

◆ Caulk any gaps between the fan and the siding.

3. Wiring the fan.

◆ Stretch out a length of flexible armored cable between the service panel and the fan, but do not connect the wiring.

◆ Slide the cable through a knockout opening in the fan junction box and anchor it with a cable clamp. With wire caps, connect the black cable wire to the black fan wire and the white cable wire to the white fan wire. Connect the bare cable wire to the fan grounding screw.

◆ Fasten the cable along the wall with armored cable straps.

◆ Have an electrician wire the cable to the service panel.

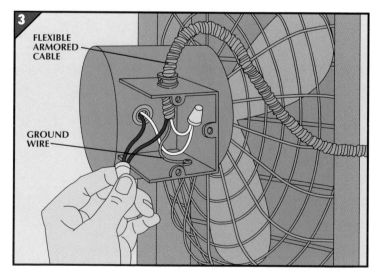

Building a Pass-Through

For safety and convenience, you need a way to move materials in and out of the shop with ease. In some cases, you may be able to rearrange furniture, fixtures, and appliances to provide access. But often, the obstacle is an immovable part of the house—a projecting wall, a narrow doorway, or a winding staircase. Threading materials through your house in these circumstances is not only inconvenient—the exercise will also track dirt and dust through the house.

A Simple Slot: For a shop on the ground floor, you can frame an opening through an exterior wall. To accommodate unwieldy items such as 4-by-8 panels, the portal need only be 55 inches high and 6 to 8 inches wide *(below and page 20)*. Locating the opening between two adjoining studs takes little carpentry skill and entails no risk to the structure of your house.

 TOOLS

Electronic stud sensor
Carpenter's level
Compass saw
Circular saw
Hammer
Electric drill
Screwdriver
Nail set
Paintbrush
Caulking gun

 MATERIALS

2 x 4s
Sill stock
Shims
Common nails ($3\frac{1}{2}$")
Plywood ($\frac{3}{4}$")
Offset hinges
Door-stop molding
Galvanized finishing nails ($1\frac{1}{2}$", 2", $2\frac{1}{2}$")
Spring catches
Security hasp
Weather stripping
Wallboard repair materials
Molding
Drip edge
Paint
Caulk

 **SAFETY TIPS**

Wear goggles when nailing or operating power tools. Put on gloves and long sleeves when handling fiberglass insulation.

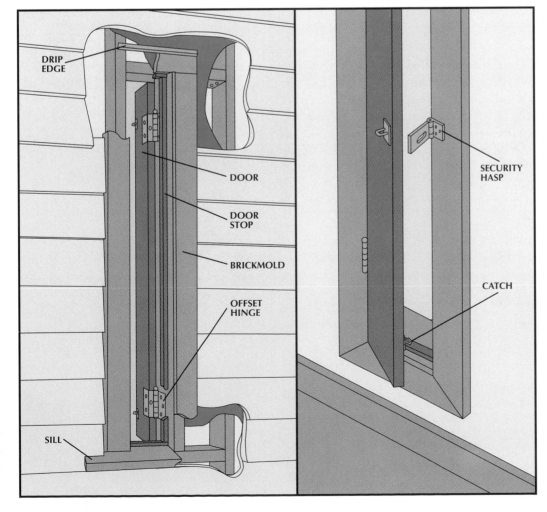

DRIP EDGE

DOOR

DOOR STOP

BRICKMOLD

OFFSET HINGE

SILL

SECURITY HASP

CATCH

A narrow portal.
A vertical opening framed between adjoining studs can accommodate 4-by-8 panels and unwieldy pieces of lumber. The door is hung on $\frac{3}{4}$-inch offset hinges. Spring-action catches, screwed to the door and the stud on one side of the pass-through, keep the door shut; weather stripping attached to the door stops blocks drafts. Casing is installed around the opening on the inside *(near left)*. Outside, brickmold frames the sides and top; a drip edge is added at the top, and a sloping sill is installed along the bottom of the opening *(far left)*. All exposed wood is painted, and caulk is applied where trim meets siding. A security hasp installed on the inside permits the door to be padlocked.

A WALL SLOT FOR PLYWOOD

1. Framing the opening.
◆ Turn off electrical power to the work area, then mark and cut an opening through the interior wall between two studs, starting 4 to 8 inches above the baseboard and extending 55 inches up the wall; take care not to cut into any wires. Remove insulation from the opening.
◆ Cut two 2-by-4s to fit between the studs. With $3\frac{1}{2}$-inch common nails, toenail the 2-by-4s to the studs across the top and bottom of the opening.
◆ Cut a third 2-by-4 to fit vertically between the first two boards, then toenail it in place 7 inches from one stud and 6 inches from the other (left).
◆ Drill a hole at each corner of the 7-inch slot through the exterior wall; then working outside, cut the opening defined by the drilled holes.

2. Hanging the door.
◆ To make the door, cut a piece of $\frac{3}{4}$-inch plywood to fit inside the 7-inch-wide opening.
◆ Fasten two offset hinges to the door, then secure them to the vertical 2-by-4 (right).
◆ Close the door, then cut pieces of door-stop molding to fit around the sides and top. With $1\frac{1}{2}$-inch finishing nails, fasten the stops to the frame around the door.
◆ Cut a length of commercial sill stock 7 inches long plus the width of the pieces of brick-mold to be applied. Notch the sill at each end so it fits inside the 7-inch opening on top of the lower 2-by-4 and just touches the closed door. Shim it to slope toward the outside and fasten it to the 2-by-4 with $2\frac{1}{2}$-inch finishing nails. Cut door-stop molding to run along the edge butting against the door, and fasten it in place.
◆ Mount two spring-action catches on the inside of the door near the free edge—one at the top and one at the bottom. Fasten the strikes to the door and the catches to the stop (inset). Then screw on a security hasp, and attach weather stripping to the door stops.
◆ Replace the insulation in the open half of the slot, then patch the opening with wallboard.
◆ Inside and out, frame the opening with molding fastened with 2-inch finishing nails, using wood strips to bring it flush with the walls if necessary. Outside add drip edge between the siding and the top piece of molding. Paint all the exposed wood and caulk the gaps between the siding and the molding.

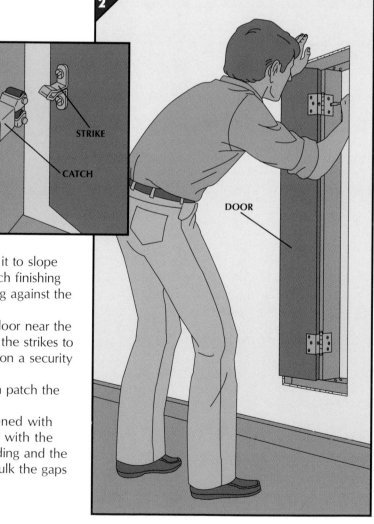

STRIKE

CATCH

DOOR

Noisy workshops are much more than just an annoyance to others. Continued exposure to noise can damage your hearing and promote fatigue—a leading cause of accidents in the workshop.

Protecting Your Hearing: Guard yourself from the harmful effects of noise by wearing hearing protection. Earmuffs are effective, but earplugs are less expensive and more comfortable, particularly when paired with goggles. To minimize vibrations produced by tools, place neoprene isolation mounts under machines or the legs of tool stands *(below)*. Install acoustic ceiling tiles to soften reverberations.

Containing Noise: To reduce the passage of noise to adjoining living areas, prevent it from passing through solid materials, such as wallboard and wood, and through the air with sound-reduction strategies. These measures block both routes at once by creating as wide and dense a barrier as possible between rooms and by isolating barrier parts from each other so the sound cannot travel across them.

To prevent noises from traveling from an attic to the story below, install a double-thickness floor that separates the attic floor from the joists under it *(page 22, top)*. Added fiberglass insulation will help buffer noise.

To keep sound in lower-floor shops from traveling sideways or upward, insulate walls and ceilings, then separate the wallboard from studs and joists with resilient channels or Z-furring strips *(pages 22-23)*. For an even more effective sound barrier between rooms, you can erect special walls built with staggered studs.

To block noise from passing room to room through the air, seal small openings between rooms with silicone caulk, weather stripping, or special duct liners *(page 23)*.

 TOOLS

Electric drill
Screwdriver

Hammer
Circular saw
Utility knife

  MATERIALS

Antivibration pads
Stove bolts
Rubber washers
Fiberglass insulation
Plywood ($\frac{1}{2}$")
Fiberboard ($\frac{1}{2}$")
Roofing nails ($1\frac{1}{2}$")
Wood glue

2 x 3s, 2 x 4s, 2 x 6s
Resilient channels
Z-furring
Wallboard materials
Drywall screws ($1\frac{1}{2}$", 2")
Acoustic tiles
Weather stripping
Door sweep
Duct-lining kit

 **SAFETY TIPS**

Wear goggles when driving nails or operating power tools. Don goggles, a dust mask, gloves, and a long-sleeved shirt to handle fiberglass insulation.

REDUCING NOISE AT THE SOURCE

Minimizing vibration.
◆ With the tool in its usual position, mark its bolt holes, and drill a hole through the worktable at each mark.
◆ Stack a pair of antivibration pads without interlocking the grooves and drill a hole through them.
◆ Place the pads over the holes in the worktable, set the tool on the pads, and fasten it in place with stove bolts, adding rubber washers on each side *(inset)*.

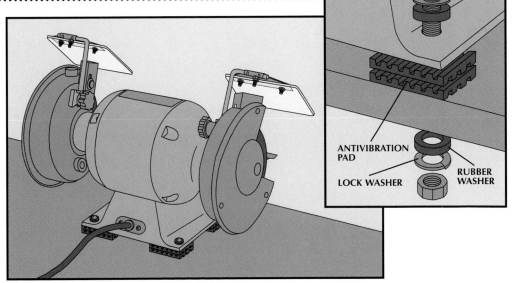

ANTIVIBRATION PAD

LOCK WASHER

RUBBER WASHER

A BUILT-UP BARRIER UNDERFOOT

Building a soundproof floor.

◆ If possible, install batts of 3-inch fiberglass insulation between the joists below the floor.

◆ Over a $\frac{1}{2}$-inch plywood subfloor, place $\frac{1}{2}$-inch resilient fiberboard, fastened to the joists with $1\frac{1}{2}$-inch roofing nails.

◆ Using only wood glue, fasten 2-by-3 furring strips to the fiberboard centered between the joists.

◆ Nail a layer of $\frac{1}{2}$-inch plywood over the furring strips and top the plywood with a floor covering such as sheet vinyl.

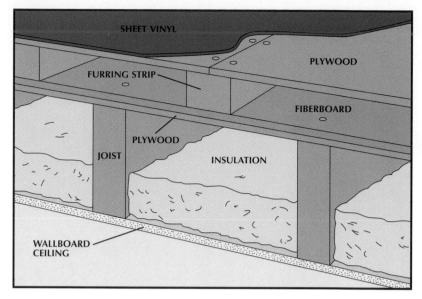

SOUND-DEADENING WALLS AND CEILINGS

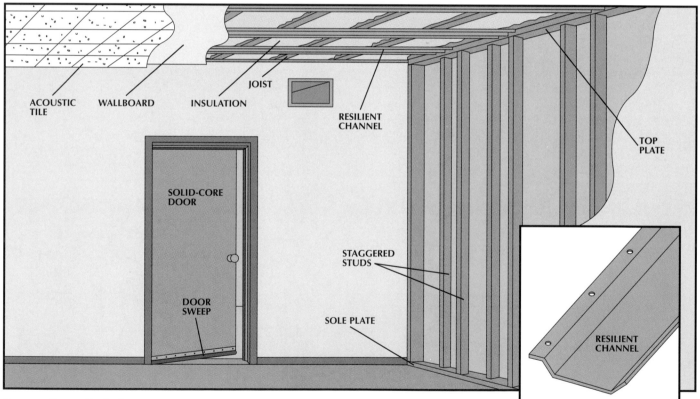

A soundproofed shop.

Several soundproofing techniques can be built into a shop (above). Fiberglass insulation is stapled between ceiling joists. Running perpendicular to the joists, resilient metal channels (inset) separate the joists from the ceiling wallboard. The nar-row flanges of the channels are screwed to the joists, and the wallboard is fastened to the wide section with $1\frac{1}{2}$-inch drywall screws. Walls can be soundproofed like the ceilings or a new wall can be built with 2-by-6 top and sole plates, and 2-by-4 studs positioned in a W pattern to the plates, placed so the centers of the studs are 2 feet apart. A solid-core door blocks sound, and unless the heating system requires airflow underneath the door, a door sweep and weather stripping seal any gaps around the door.

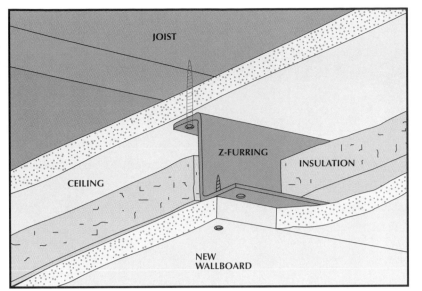

Soundproofing a finished ceiling.

◆ With 2-inch drywall screws, fasten the narrow flanges of 2-inch-deep Z-furring through the ceiling to the joists above.

◆ Attach a layer of wallboard to the wide flanges of the strips, inserting 1-inch-thick sheets of fiberglass insulation as you go.

◆ Glue acoustic tiles to the new ceiling to dampen reverberations in the shop.

PLUGGING HOLES THAT TRANSMIT SOUND

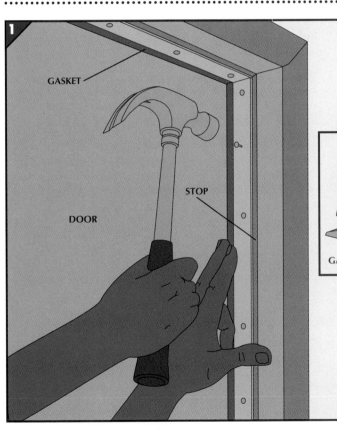

1. Sealing around doors.

◆ Cut lengths of weather stripping to fit around the perimeter of the door.

◆ Hold each piece flat against the stop so the gasket is partly compressed against the door. Secure the strip to the stop with the nails provided *(left)*.

◆ To seal the gap under the door, install a sweep on the bottom of the door so the gasket is slightly compressed when the door is closed against the threshold *(inset)*. You may need to trim the door to get the right fit.

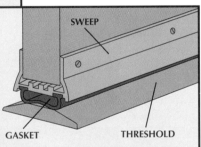

2. Installing duct liners.

◆ Unscrew the grille over the duct opening, then reach in and measure as far up the duct as you can.

◆ Cut acoustic duct liner to fit the measured areas and coat exposed surfaces with the adhesive sold by the liner manufacturer. Apply adhesive to the unbacked side of each piece of liner and press it into position inside the duct.

◆ Let the adhesive dry, check that the pieces are secure, then replace the grille.

Equipping the Shop for Action

A functional workshop has three fundamental requirements: a complement of tools, sufficient lighting, and enough electricity to power both. Once you have selected the portable and stationary tools suited to your needs and have laid them out efficiently, you'll need to route electrical power through the shop—both to serve the tools and shed light on the work at hand.

Creating a path for electrical cable →

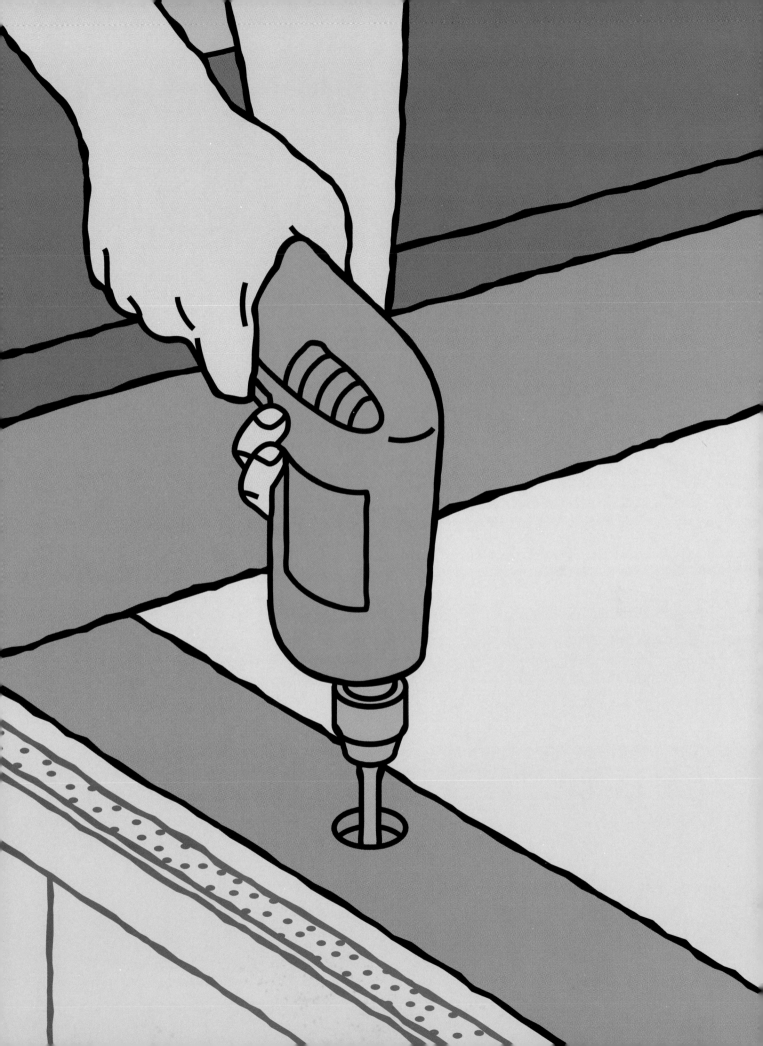

One of the first tasks in preparing a workshop for action is to take an inventory of the tools you have, and decide what additional ones you require *(chart, pages 28-29).*

Choosing Tools: The key to selecting tools is quality—each type requires certain features to perform properly *(below and opposite).* Look for reputable brand names. Before buying, check performance tests in do-it-yourself and consumer magazines so you can confine your search to tools that have been given high ratings. Inspect the item before buying it. Quality products have a solid feel and a finely worked finish. Although such tools are seldom available at bargain-basement prices, they are designed to provide decades of service.

Buying Tools: To guard against impulse purchases of items you are unlikely to ever need, draw up a purchase plan and stick to it; or, simply wait until you actually need a tool, then buy the best-quality model you can afford. Watch for sales, but confirm that the price includes the normal warranty. To save money, buy tools in sets—screwdrivers, chisels, and wrenches, for example, are less expensive when purchased this way, although your initial investment will be higher than for a smaller number of individual items. Don't exclude garage sales and country auctions, where you may be able to find rock-bottom prices, but examine the merchandise with care.

Chisels.
Four wood chisels with blades ranging in width from $\frac{1}{4}$ to 1 inch suffice for most jobs. Look for high-impact plastic handles and a washer between the blade and the handle to act as a shock absorber. For chopping mortises, you will need a set of firmer chisels. For metalwork, choose a cold chisel with a flat $\frac{1}{2}$-inch blade. For splitting bricks, buy a brick set.

Clamps.
There are dozens of clamp designs for securing workpieces and tools, each type suited to a particular purpose, but a collection of C-clamps can see you through most jobs. Useful additions include wooden screw clamps. Because their jaws can be adjusted to a wide range of angles, they are more versatile than C-clamps. Bar clamps are essential for securing large projects, and web clamps wrap around odd-shaped pieces like chairs. Quick clamps, with their one fixed jaw and one sliding jaw, and spring clamps are easy to use.

Files and rasps.
Designed to trim metal and wood, the basic half-round file is 10 inches long, with rows of coarse bladelike ridges on the rounded side and criss-crossed, or "double-cut," ridges on the flat side. A patternmaker's cabinet rasp has irregularly placed teeth that make the tool easy to control when shaping wood. More specialized files and rasps include flat, round, and triangular types for trimming odd-shaped work. Two helpful accessories are a wood or plastic handle that can be switched from file to file as needed, and a stiff-wire brush—called a file card—for cleaning shavings from file teeth.

Handsaws.
For most carpentry projects, a combination saw for cutting both with and across the grain is most practical. Look for a polished blade to reduce friction as it passes through wood. Make sure the teeth are sharp and uniform in shape and size, and that the handle feels comfortable and solid. Other useful saws include the backsaw, which is used in a miter box for angled cuts, and the coping saw and the compass saw for cutting curves.

Manual drilling tools.
The "egg-beater" drill is ideal for boring holes up to $\frac{1}{4}$ inch in diameter; choose one with metal rather than plastic gears. A push drill with a ratchet mechanism bores pilot holes for screws and small holes in delicate work. The brace-and-bit type can drive bits that are too large for most $\frac{3}{8}$-inch electric drills. Buy one with a reversible ratchet for work in tight areas.

Hammers.

A curved-claw hammer excels at pulling nails, but a straight-claw hammer is more useful for prying boards apart. The tempered head of a ball-peen hammer is meant for striking cold chisels and other metal tools. The best heads are made of drop-forged steel, seamless, and highly polished. Buy a weight that suits the job and feels comfortable; for general carpentry, a 16-ounce model is the most common. Finish work calls for a lighter hammer, while a heavier one is needed for rough construction.

Measuring and marking tools.

A flexible steel measuring tape in a sturdy case is invaluable. Buy a tape marked in both incremental and cumulative feet and inches, and with 16-inch intervals highlighted to help locate stud positions. A 6-foot folding extension ruler with a brass inset that slides out for measuring inside dimensions is handy. Levels should feature metal bodies or metal edges and replaceable vials. A marking gauge is useful for scribing lines along the edge of a board.

Screwdrivers.

Every tool collection needs at least four common sizes of flat-tip screwdrivers, and two sizes of Phillips screwdrivers. You may want to add screwdrivers for square-drive screws. Ensure that the tip and shaft are made of chrome-vanadium steel. A plastic handle with a rubber cover makes the best shock insulator for electrical work. You'll also find a collection of screwdriver bits for use in a variable-speed drill.

Wrenches and sockets.

The most versatile wrench is the 10-inch adjustable wrench with smooth jaws. Buy one made of drop-forged steel with a chrome finish. If you plan on doing even a modest amount of mechanical work, you will need a set of fixed-width wrenches. Open-end wrenches slip around nuts and boltheads from the side, while box wrenches fit over nuts and bolts and are especially suited to hexagonal nuts and boltheads. Combination wrenches combine the two types, but separate sets of open-end and box wrenches may be more convenient, especially when two wrenches of the same size are needed at one time. Socket wrenches, driven by handles with ratchet mechanisms, speed the task of tightening bolts and facilitate working in tight spots. A good basic set has a $\frac{3}{8}$-inch-wide drive post and hexagonal sockets. Buy metric-standard wrenches if you will work on foreign bicycles or cars.

Hand planes.

The block plane, for trimming end grain, and the smoothing plane, for shaving with the grain, are the two essential planing tools. Choose models with flat soles and high-quality steel blades. The best-quality planes have adjustment mechanisms that hold their positions and allow exact control over the amount of wood to be shaved. For keeping the blades razor-sharp, you'll need a 4000x whetstone and a honing guide.

Pliers.

A pair of 8-inch slip-joint pliers is needed for bending and gripping. Diagonal-cutting pliers snip wire and small nails. A pair of locking-grip pliers can be adjusted to clamp onto an object, serving as a wrench. Long-nose pliers can reach into recessed areas and are especially handy for making terminal loops on electrical wires. Look for those made of chrome-plated steel with strong joints and plastic-coated handles.

Portable power tools.

Small power tools, such as a $\frac{3}{8}$-inch electric drill and a $7\frac{1}{4}$-inch circular saw, have become an indispensable part of most workshops. Other useful electric tools include a saber saw, a router, and belt and random-orbit sanders. When purchasing portable power tools, buy items of at least medium quality. Check for plastic double-insulated bodies, heavy-duty power cords, and permanently lubricated bearings. Models with variable-speed control are convenient. Drills, circular saws, and screwdrivers are available in handy cordless versions as well.

THE RIGHT TOOL FOR THE JOB

The chart below and opposite rates the suitability of a wide range of hand and power tools in six categories of projects. To determine whether you are likely to need a tool, check whether it is deemed essential "E" or desirable "D" in the appropriate category. Keep in mind that these ratings are not the last word in tool selection. Certain projects straddle two or more categories, and no two jobs are ever exactly the same.

Tools	Basic Household Maintenance	Plumbing	Electrical	Masonry	Carpentry	Woodworking
CHISELS						
Brick set				E		
Cold chisel	D	D		E		
Wood chisel	D		D		E	E
CLAMPS						
Bar clamp					E	E
C-clamp	E				E	E
Screw clamp						E
CUTTING TOOLS						
Backsaw and miter box		D			E	E
Coping saw	D				E	E
Combination saw	E				E	E
Compass saw	D	E	E		D	
Dovetail saw					D	E
Hacksaw	E	E			D	
Pipe cutter		E	E			
Tin snips	D		D			
Utility knife	E	E	E		D	
Wire stripper			E			
DRILLING TOOLS (Manual)						
Brace and bit					D	D
Hand drill	D				D	E
Push drill	D					D
FILES						
Flat file	D					
Rasp					E	E
Round and half-round files	E					D
Triangular file					D	
HAMMERS						
Ball-peen hammer	E	D		E		
Bricklayer's hammer		D		E		
Claw hammer	E	E	D	E	E	E
MEASURING AND MARKING						
Awl					E	E
Carpenter's square	D			E	E	E
Chalk line				E	E	
Combination square	E				E	E
Folding ruler	D				E	E
Level	E	E		E	E	D

E=Essential   D=Desirable

Tools	Basic Household Maintenance	Plumbing	Electrical	Masonry	Carpentry	Woodworking
MEASURING AND MARKING						
Marking gauge					D	E
Tape measure	E	E	E	E	E	E
MISCELLANEOUS						
Bench vise		E			E	E
File card						D
Nail set	D				E	E
Plunger	E	E				
Pointing trowel				E		
Propane torch		E				
Pry bar	E			D	E	
Putty knife	E				E	D
Staple gun	E		D		D	
Star drill				E		
Voltage tester	D		E			
Whetstone	D				E	E
PLANES						
Block plane	E				E	E
Smoothing plane	D				E	E
Rabbet plane						D
PLIERS						
Channel-lock pliers		E				
Diagonal-cutting pliers	D		E			
Locking-grip pliers	E	E	D		E	
Long-nose pliers	D	E	E			
Slip-joint pliers	E	E			E	D
PORTABLE POWER TOOLS						
Belt sander					D	E
Circular saw	E				E	D
Electric drill	E	E	E	E	E	E
Random-orbit sander	D				D	E
Router					D	E
Saber saw	D		D		E	D
SCREWDRIVERS						
Flat-tip screwdrivers	E	E	E		E	E
Offset screwdrivers			D			D
Phillips-head screwdrivers	E	E	E			D
Square-drive screwdrivers	D	D	D			D
WRENCHES						
Adjustable wrench	E	E			E	D
Basin wrench		E				
Box and open-end wrenches	D				D	
Pipe wrench		E				
Socket wrench	D	E			D	
Spud wrench		E				

E=Essential   **D**=Desirable

With their power and precision, stationary tools increase the versatility and efficiency of a shop, but they also carry hefty price tags. Before buying any, consider the amount and kind of work you do as well as the available floor space in your shop.

Tool Selection: Most shop work with power tools involves cutting wood. Drilling, joining, smoothing, and finishing compose most of the remaining tasks. If this is your situation, you can make a table saw or a radial-arm saw the centerpiece of your shop.

Although the table saw *(below)* is the preferred tool for cutting plywood panels and making precise joinery cuts, the radial-arm saw *(page 32)* is more versatile—it can sand and plane wood as well as cut it. The radial-arm saw is also easier to set up for making repetitive cuts.

If your projects entail curved cuts, a band saw *(page 34)* is essential. Hobbyists may prefer a scroll saw; its fine blade can cut intricate shapes in lightweight materials. A drill press is a valuable addition *(page 35)*; it not only bores holes accurately, but doubles as a sander and a mortiser. A jointer and a planer *(page 36)* will enable you to smooth rough-cut boards. If you want to turn wood, as in bowl making or spindle work, you'll need a lathe *(page 37)*.

Budgeting: If your shop space is limited, consider a compact multi-purpose shop tool that combines the functions of several individual machines *(pages 38-39)*. Although expensive, it may cost less than the total price of the tools it replaces; however, setting it up for different functions can be time-consuming.

If your budget is tight, choose the most versatile tools, such as the radial-arm saw and the drill press, and add accessories as needed. Or, purchase secondhand tools—provided you try them out first.

THE TABLE SAW

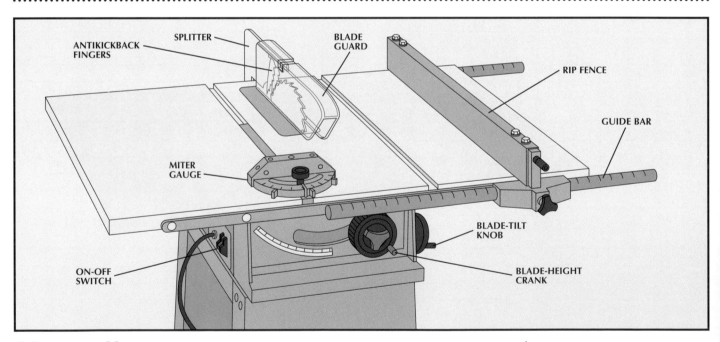

Sizing up a table saw.
This tool provides a flat, stationary surface on which materials can be accurately guided over a rotating circular blade that projects through a slot in the table top. It can execute a wide range of cuts, including rips, crosscuts, miters, and compound angles. Most table saws

accommodate a 10-inch blade that can be raised or lowered to adjust the cutting depth, or tilted to cut a bevel.

Look for a table wide enough for the rip fence to be set at least 24 inches from the blade; add-on table extensions are usually available to support extra-large work.

A $1\frac{1}{2}$- to 3-horsepower motor with a speed of 3450 rpm is adequate for home-workshop use.

Vital to the table saw are its safety features: a plastic or metal blade guard, a splitting device to keep the wood from binding on the blade, and anti-kickback fingers.

TABLE-SAW BLADES AND ACCESSORIES

To make the most of a table saw, outfit it with a full complement of blades and special cutting tools. The blade sold with most saws is a combination blade designed to work efficiently on both crosscuts—across the wood grain—or on rip cuts—along the wood grain, although specialized blades for each of these cuts are available. For cleaner edges and a narrower kerf, use a hollow-ground blade; its teeth are set directly in line with the body of the blade, which is thinner than its cutting edge. Plywood and laminate blades, designed for these materials, make smooth cuts with less splintering or damage to the layers.

For cutting rabbets and dadoes—the rectangular channels employed in woodworking joints—the saw takes a dado head, which consists of two circular blades assembled around a variable number of inner blades called chippers. The chippers cut away wood between the two main blades. On quality dado heads the main blades are hollow ground. For more intricate cuts, a molding cutterhead is used as a mount for three identically contoured blades that are fastened into it with screws. Except for hollow-ground blades, all these can be purchased with carbide tips. Though more expensive, they stay sharper much longer.

DADO HEAD

BLADES

THIS SIDE OUT
3" x 24; ½" Bore

COMBINATION BLADE

CROSSCUT BLADE

RIP BLADE

PLYWOOD BLADE

LAMINATE BLADE

MOLDING CUTTERHEAD

CHIPPER

ROLLER ASSEMBLY

Accommodating a table saw.

For rip cutting, you need adequate space both in front of and behind the table for the full length of the board *(left)*. To support the cut sections as they come through the saw, you can clamp a roller assembly to a sawhorse, or buy or make a roller stand *(page 86)*. For crosscutting, make room on each side of the table to accommodate the workpiece.

A VERSATILE ALTERNATIVE: THE RADIAL-ARM SAW

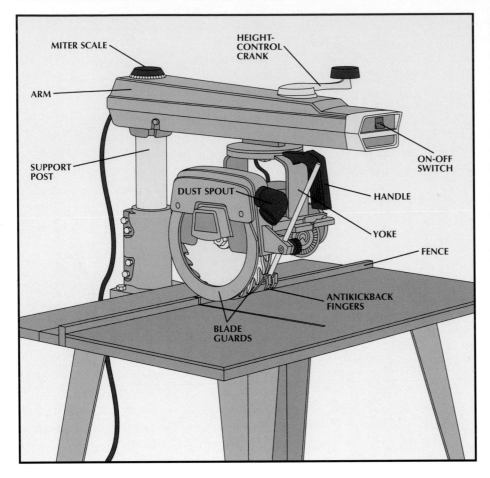

MITER SCALE

HEIGHT-CONTROL CRANK

ARM

ON-OFF SWITCH

SUPPORT POST

DUST SPOUT

HANDLE

YOKE

FENCE

ANTIKICKBACK FINGERS

BLADE GUARDS

Selecting a radial-arm saw.

Except when executing rip cuts, the blade of a radial-arm saw moves while the wood remains stationary. The blade, held in a yoke, rides along a track, tilts 90 degrees right or left, and swivels 360 degrees beneath a support arm that is adjustable both laterally and vertically. These capabilities give the saw much of the mobility and flexibility of a portable power saw; however, all these variables can make the radial arm saw difficult to adjust with precision.

A typical radial-arm saw for the home workshop has a blade 10 inches in diameter. It cuts to a maximum depth of 3 inches, crosscuts boards 13 inches wide, and rips wood up to $24\frac{1}{2}$ inches wide. Look for a saw with a heavy-duty arm-and-support-post assembly and a motor rating of at least 2 horse-power. An automatic or manual brake is also important. Other desirable features are floating blade guards and adjustable antikickback fingers for protection during ripping.

Accessories.

The radial-arm saw accepts the same types of blades as a table saw, including dado blades *(page 31)*, but because the blade rotates toward the workpiece in most operations, the saw may "self-feed" through the wood. To prevent this, use only blades whose teeth have a maximum hook angle of 5 degrees, as labeled on the package.

By removing the standard circular blade and tilting the saw's motor in its yoke, you can fit the tool with a number of accessories. A drum sander lets you use the saw's spinning action to smooth wood edges *(right)*; clamp on an auxiliary table cut from plywood and notched to provide a raised surface for the workpiece so the drum contacts its entire edge. Molding cutterheads *(page 31)* can be used, but the saw will need a special blade guard. A sanding disk can be added *(photograph, left)*; and for certain planing tasks, such as cutting wide bevels on the surface of a raised panel, the radial-arm saw can be fitted with a circular planing attachment *(photograph, right)*.

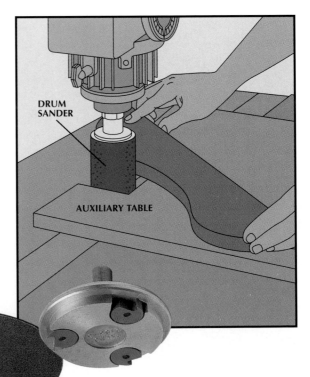

DRUM SANDER

AUXILIARY TABLE

Making space for the saw.

Unlike a table saw, the radial-arm saw can be backed against a workshop wall. In rip cutting, the blade is set sideways; in crosscutting *(right)*, the lumber is lined up against the fence at the back of the table and the yoke is pulled forward along its arm to make the cut, then returned behind the fence. The machine itself occupies roughly 6 square feet and requires a few feet of maneuvering space in front for its operator; however, you will also need sufficient space on both sides—ideally 10 to 12 feet—to accommodate long pieces of lumber. Worktables on either side of the saw are useful for supporting long boards.

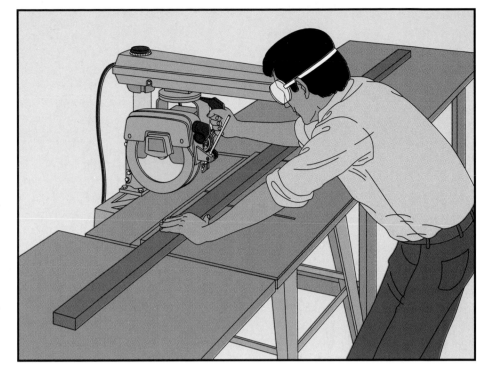

THE SLIDING COMPOUND-MITER SAW

This tool is ideal for making precision miter, bevel, and compound cuts. Since the arm and table rotate as a unit, setting accurate angles is easy. The tool can crosscut and bevel stock up to 12 inches wide, and make miter and compound cuts in stock up to $8\frac{1}{2}$ inches wide. It features an $8\frac{1}{2}$-inch blade that runs along a slide, and an electric brake to stop the blade spinning quickly when the trigger is released.

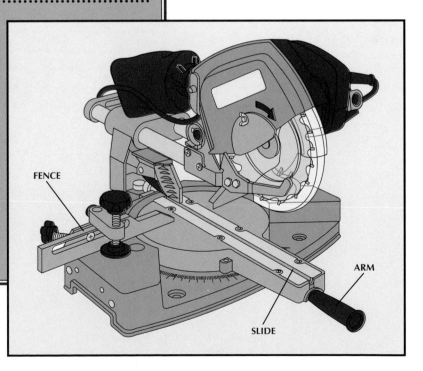

FENCE

ARM

SLIDE

SAWS THAT CUT CURVES

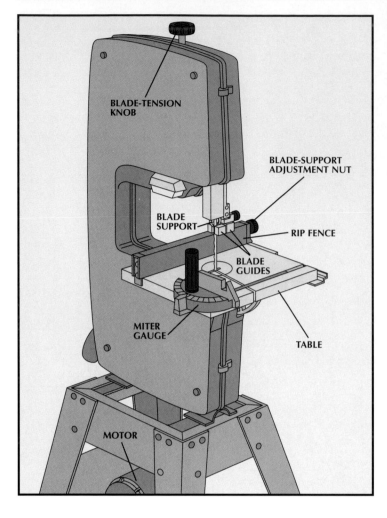

BLADE-TENSION KNOB

BLADE-SUPPORT ADJUSTMENT NUT

BLADE SUPPORT

RIP FENCE

BLADE GUIDES

MITER GAUGE

TABLE

MOTOR

The band saw.

Prized for its ability to cut curved lines and for its unmatched depth of cut, a band saw has a continuous blade driven in one direction around two wheels, one above the other, encased in a metal housing. Only the section of blade above the worktable is exposed. Because the blade pulls the workpiece toward the table, kickback cannot occur. The size of a band saw is determined by its throat, the distance between the blade and the vertical arm at the tool's back; its capacity is rated by maximum depth of cut. An average home tool has a throat of 10 to 14 inches and will cut through wood 6 inches thick. Most home band saws have $\frac{1}{2}$- to 1-horsepower motors and take blades from $\frac{1}{8}$ to $\frac{1}{2}$ inch wide with a variety of teeth configurations for different materials and types of cut.

Look for a band saw table that tilts to 45 degrees so you can make bevel cuts. Guide bars for a rip fence and a miter gauge will allow you to rip boards and make a range of cross-grain cuts.

Band saws do not take up much space, but you will need enough room to maneuver materials.

The scroll saw.

Sometimes called a jig saw, the scroll saw can make intricate cuts in thin material. The slender blades are held between two chucks on either side of the table. For the home shop, this type of saw needs a cutting depth of about 2 inches. Throat depth ranges from 13 to 30 inches. Scroll-saw motors are generally rated at $\frac{1}{3}$ horsepower; look for one that has at least two speeds. Other useful features are a tilting table, built-in lights, spring-loaded guards that hold the work against the table, and blowers that keep the cutting area clear of sawdust.

The blades are available with different tooth configurations and thicknesses that enable you to cut diverse materials like wood, plastic, and soft metals; spiral blades are designed for cutting tight curves (*photograph*).

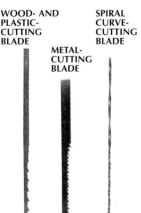

WOOD- AND PLASTIC-CUTTING BLADE

METAL-CUTTING BLADE

SPIRAL CURVE-CUTTING BLADE

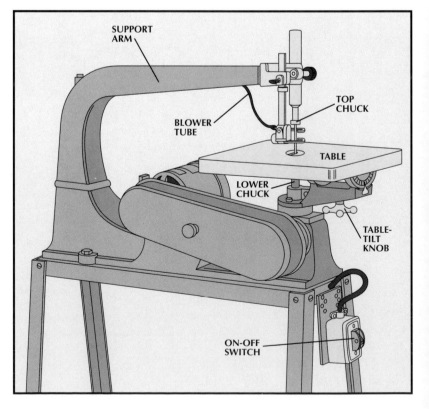

SUPPORT ARM

BLOWER TUBE

TOP CHUCK

TABLE

LOWER CHUCK

TABLE-TILT KNOB

ON-OFF SWITCH

THE DRILL PRESS

Sizing it up.

A drill press cuts perfect circular openings as much as 6 inches in diameter; with accessories *(below)*, it can do much more. Drill-press capacity is determined by the distance from the column to the center of the spindle—typically 7 inches. The table slides up and down the column to adjust the distance between the tabletop and the chuck.

The spindle of the press is covered by a metal sleeve known as a quill. The quill is lowered by means of a feed lever to drill holes of varying depth, the maximum depth depending on the distance the quill travels. Quill travel ranges from $2\frac{1}{2}$ to $4\frac{1}{2}$ inches for home workshop models. An adjustable depth stop limits the quill's extension. Select a drill press that has spring action to return the quill to the starting point. Motor sizes vary from $\frac{1}{3}$ to $\frac{1}{2}$ horsepower, but the real key to a drill's versatility is its range of speeds. Most drill presses have five to six speeds that are adjusted by a step-pulley system.

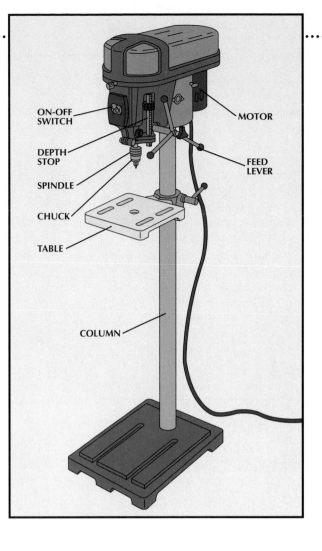

ON-OFF SWITCH

MOTOR

DEPTH STOP

FEED LEVER

SPINDLE

CHUCK

TABLE

COLUMN

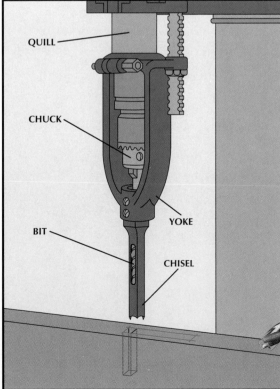

QUILL

CHUCK

BIT

YOKE

CHISEL

Accessories.

A mortising attachment, with a yoke that clamps on the drill-press quill *(left)*, creates crisp, clean mortises. The yoke holds a square, hollow chisel that forms the corners of the mortise, while the augerlike bit inside does the bulk of the cutting. In addition to common bits such as a twist bit, a spade bit, and a hole saw, a number of specialized bits are available *(photographs)*. A brad-point bit has a center point to guide the drill; the sharp spurs along the outside prevent tearout. A Forstner bit makes clean-edged, flat-bottomed holes up to 1 inch in diameter, but it is guided by its edges rather than its point, making it ideal for creating angled holes. A plug cutter produces wood plugs for concealing screw holes, and can also make short dowels. Fly cutters can make holes up to 8 inches in diameter.

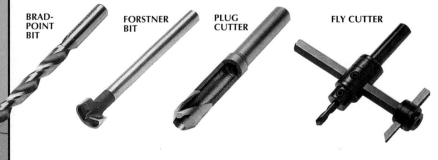

BRAD-POINT BIT

FORSTNER BIT

PLUG CUTTER

FLY CUTTER

MACHINES THAT SHAPE WOOD

Jointers.

Jointers are used to shave small amounts of wood from the edges and faces of boards, yielding smooth, even surfaces. The jointer can also cut rabbets and tenons for woodworking joints, and shape bevels and tapers. Jointers suited to home workshops have 6-inch-wide blades capable of cuts up to $\frac{3}{8}$ inch deep. Look for one with a table at least 27 inches long and a motor rated $\frac{3}{4}$ horsepower or higher. A fence that tilts in both directions is very handy. A spring-loaded guard covering the blades, which is moved aside as the workpiece is pushed through, is an essential safety feature.

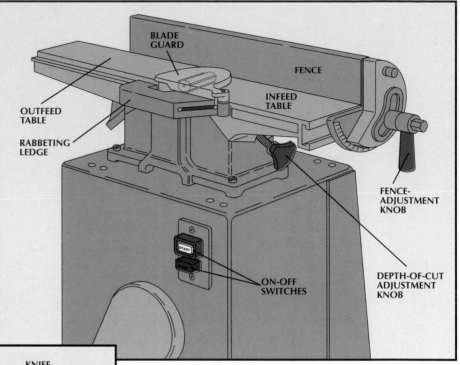

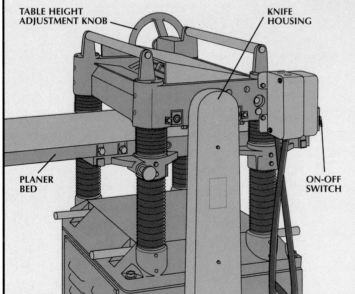

Planers.

For reducing the thickness of boards uniformly or smoothing rough lumber and glued-up panels, the planer is ideal. The machine's planer bed moves up or down to accommodate the thickness of the board. An infeed roller pushes the board into the cutterhead mounted above the bed, and an outfeed roller moves the wood out of the machine. Although the tool will produce a smooth surface that is parallel with the opposite face, it cannot straighten a warped board.

For home use, look for a planer that can handle boards up to 12 inches wide. A cast-iron planer bed and a three-blade cutterhead are desirable features.

A TABLE FOR STATIONARY ROUTING

Supporting a router upside down with its bit protruding from a hole, a router table transforms this portable tool into a stationary one. Among the tasks you can accomplish on a router table are shaping edges, plowing dadoes, and cutting woodworking joints. Look for a table with a flat top, an adjustable fence, and a miter gauge slot—or build your own (pages 92-93).

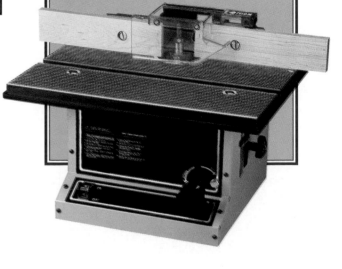

THE LATHE

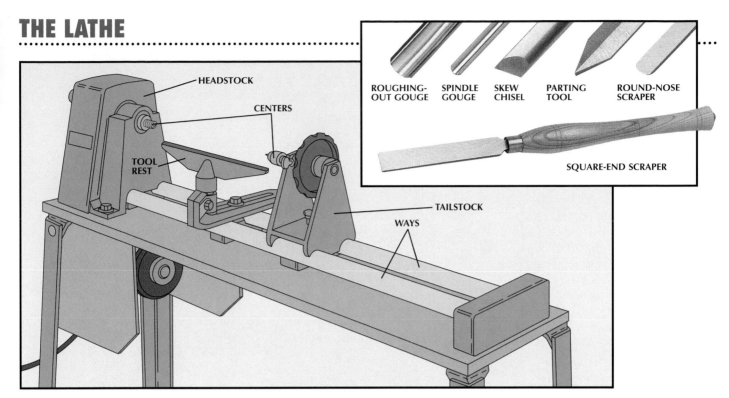

Choosing a lathe.

Unlike most shaping tools, which turn a blade, a lathe turns the wood, and the wood—known as a blank—is scraped and sheared by hand-held chisels and gouges steadied against a tool rest. For spindle turnings such as chair legs or balustrades, the wood is held between centers in the headstock and tailstock. For bowl making, work is mounted on the headstock alone. A typical home workshop lathe has a capacity of 36 inches between centers, and is powered by a $\frac{1}{2}$- to $\frac{3}{4}$-horsepower motor. For a machine that will not vibrate, look for a lathe with cast-iron headstocks and tailstocks. A basic set of lathe tools (photograph) will be sufficient to get you started.

A POWERFUL SANDER

The belt-disk sander.

This tool combines a stationary disk sander with a belt sander. The disk sander, a rotating plate of steel or aluminum faced with abrasive sanding paper ranging in width from 8 to 12 inches, is most useful for smoothing end grain, miter cuts, and curved edges. The work is supported on the table in front of the disk. Buy a model with a tilting table to facilitate sanding angled surfaces, and with a slot for a miter gauge. The belt sander runs a continuous abrasive belt around two drums. Positioned horizontally, the belt is used for sanding surfaces and lengthwise edges; for such operations, the stock rests on the belt, one of its edges braced against the stop fence. The belt can also be positioned vertically for smoothing end grain. Common belt sizes are 4-by-36 and 6-by-48 inches. A $\frac{1}{2}$- to $\frac{3}{4}$-horsepower motor is adequate for the home shop.

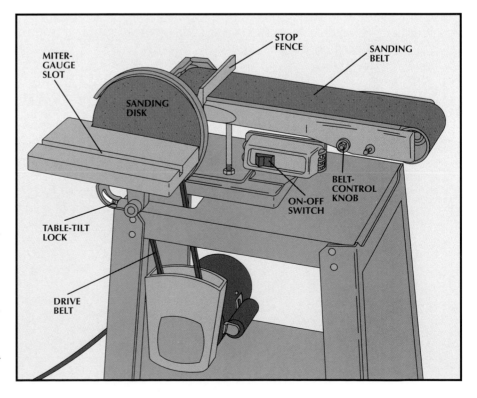

THE BENCH GRINDER

Selecting a grinder.

This relatively inexpensive tool is primarily used for sharpening the blades of other shop tools. But it is also helpful for such jobs as grinding off rivets or smoothing welded joints. The model most practical for home workshop use has a fully encased $\frac{1}{4}$- to $\frac{1}{2}$-horsepower motor and two aluminum-oxide grinding wheels fitted with covers and clear-plastic eye shields.

Home-workshop bench grinders generally have wheels ranging in diameter from 6 to 8 inches. A tool equipped with medium-coarse and medium-fine wheels is versatile enough to handle most tasks. To sharpen chisels, plane irons, and maintain other woodworking tools, add a finer 80x or 120x wheel *(photograph, left)*; a cloth buffing wheel *(photograph, right)* polishes the tool's beveled edge. An adjustable tool rest is an essential feature for this task.

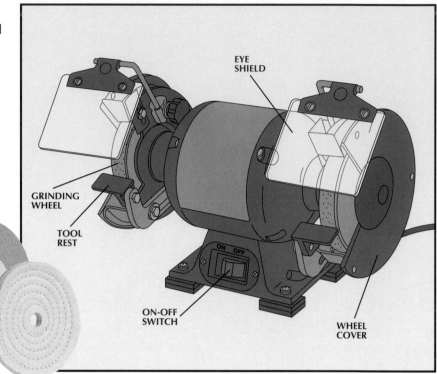

A WORKSHOP IN A SINGLE TOOL

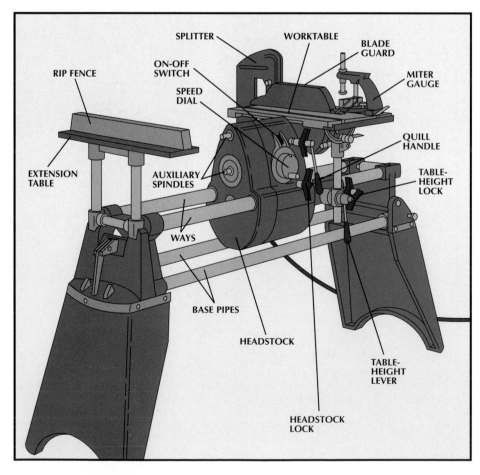

Evaluating a multipurpose tool.

An alternative to a roomful of specialized machines, a well-engineered multipurpose power tool typically occupies only 12 square feet *(left)*. Powered by a 2-horsepower variable-speed motor, and with auxiliary spindles and adjustable tubular-steel frame, this machine incorporates the capacities of five separate tools: a 10-inch table saw, a 12-inch disk sander, a $16\frac{1}{2}$-inch drill press, a 34-inch lathe, and a horizontal boring machine. With appropriate accessories, it can be further adapted for use as a band saw, saber saw, jointer, and belt sander.

Changing the tool's function involves shifting the position of the headstock and spindle, installing the proper bit, blade, or disk, and assembling the appropriate work-support jigs. The ways are also movable; normally locked horizontally, they can be tilted upright for vertical work.

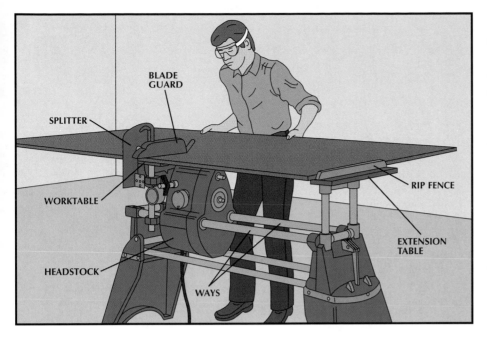

The table saw.

For sawing a wide panel *(left)*, the headstock is shifted along the ways to position the circular blade; the miter gauge is removed; and both worktable and extension table are set in place to support the wood. *(The supports for the panel behind the machine have been omitted here for the sake of clarity.)* The rip fence guides the edge of the panel as the cut is being made, and the splitter behind the blade guard keeps the cut from binding on the blade.

The lathe.

When the tool is used as a lathe *(right)*, the headstock is adjusted laterally along the ways to accommodate the length of the wood being turned. Lathe centers are attached to the drive shaft and to a tailstock attachment that locks in place at one end of the frame. The worktable and extension table are removed, and the same carriage that supports the worktable holds the tool rest to steady the chisel.

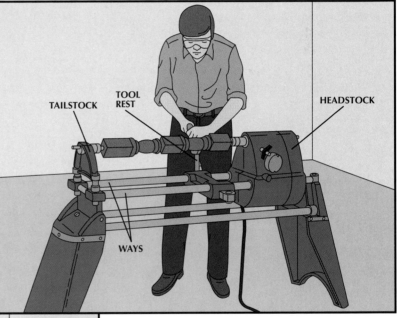

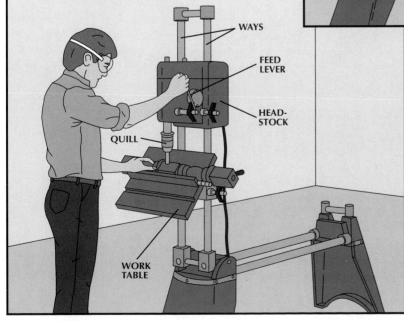

The drill press.

For use as a drill press *(left)*, the ways are tilted upright and locked in position. Both headstock and worktable are raised or lowered along these tubes to accommodate the size of the piece being drilled; the worktable also tilts to support the workpiece at any angle. As with a conventional drill press, the quill is lowered by means of a feed lever.

Tool safety is built on a foundation of caution, vigilance, and safe work habits. This precept does not only apply to novices—injuries can occur as you become more skilled if you take shortcuts and grow careless.

Know Your Machine: Carefully read the manuals that come with your power tools so you can operate them correctly. Keep tools properly adjusted and lubricated, and blades sharp. Dull blades make you force the work through the machine, which is dangerous. Unplug a machine when changing acces-sories or making major adjustments.

Get into the habit of using safety aids. Leave guards, shields, and anti-kickback devices in place. If an oper-ation makes it impossible to use them, exercise extreme caution. Use push sticks and hold-down blocks to feed and secure workpieces so your hands never come closer than 3 inches to a moving blade or sanding belt.

Electrical Safety: To avoid shocks, make sure your tools are properly grounded, and check electrical con-nections frequently for exposed or loose wires. Never stand on a wet surface while operating a power tool; keep the cord away from mov-ing blades, belts, wheels, and spin-ning shafts.

Safety Gear: Wear a face shield when using a lathe or grinding wheel; add a dust mask when you operate a belt or orbital sander. Use earplugs to protect your hear-ing. Avoid loose clothing that could catch in moving parts; tie back long hair.

Stop working when you are tired —fatigue is responsible for many ac-cidents in a home workshop.

PREVENTING SHOP ACCIDENTS

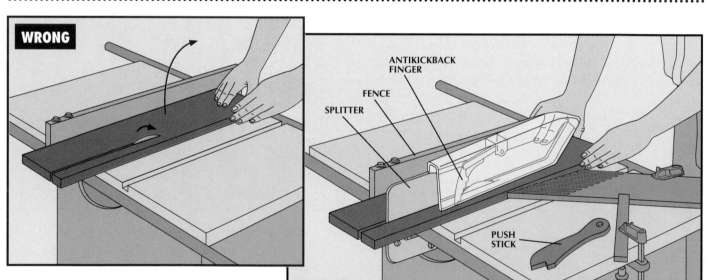

WRONG

ANTIKICKBACK FINGER

FENCE

SPLITTER

PUSH STICK

Table-saw kickback.
The kickback of a table saw can throw a piece of lumber with violence *(above, left)*. To pre-vent kickback, cut flat wood only. If you are ripping, the board requires a straight edge to ride along the rip fence. Most table-saw blade guards are equipped with a splitter and anti-kickback fingers; featherboards *(page 90)* also significantly reduce the risk of kickback by keeping the workpiece pressed against the table and rip fence. Mounted on the fence,

hold-down devices have rubber wheels that keep a workpiece firmly against the table; to prevent kickback, the wheels lock when pushed against the direction of cut, keeping the board from shooting backward. To rip a board, hold it down and push it against the fence with your left hand while your right hand—straddling the fence—moves it forward *(above, right)*. Contin-ue to feed the workpiece past the blade with a push stick *(page 90)* to keep fingers at least 3 inches away from blade.

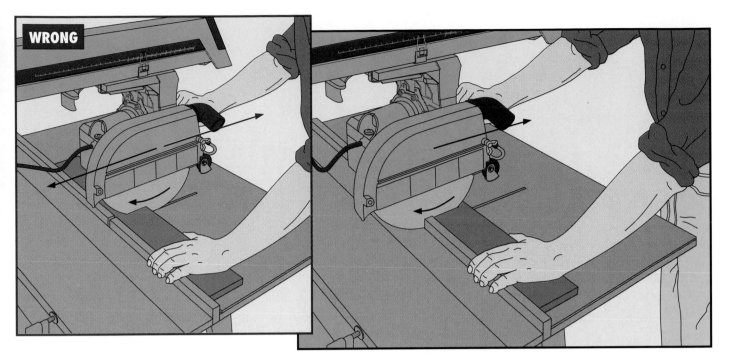

Radial-arm kickback.

To prevent self-feeding, install the correct blade *(page 32)*. If you push the blade through the wood you risk kickback, which will cause the saw to lurch toward you *(above, left)*. Instead, pull the saw through the workpiece *(above, right)*. After the cut, slide the blade back behind the fence. To make a rip cut, turn the blade parallel to the fence and lock it in position; then feed the wood into the blade, using hold-downs and anti-kickback fingers to secure it. Feed the work-piece with a push stick once your fingers are within 6 inches of the blade.

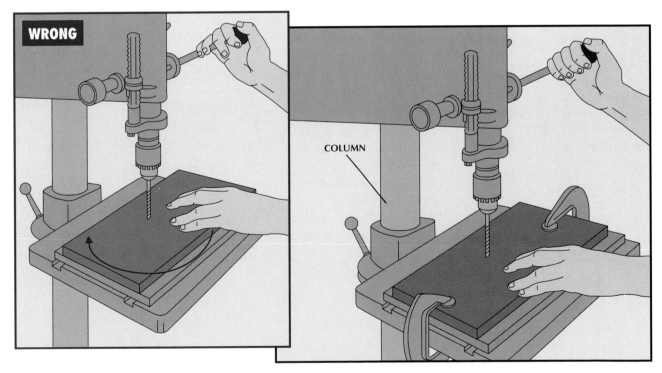

COLUMN

Drill-press twirl.

The spinning bit of a drill press can twist the workpiece right out of your hands *(above, left)*. To prevent this, brace the work against the machine's vertical back column, or anchor it with clamps at the table edges *(above, right)*; always clamp small workpieces.

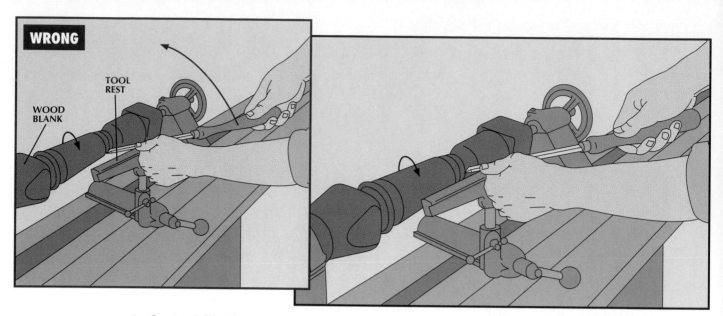

Lathe-tool flipping.

If the tool rest is too far away from the work-piece, the chisel or gouge can easily be grabbed by the wood. The tool will invariably dig into the wood and, if the tool is extended far enough, it could be flipped upward *(above, left)*. To prevent this, keep the tool rest about $\frac{1}{4}$ inch away from the workpiece, moving it closer as the blank is reduced in diameter *(above, right)*. When roughing out a square blank, start at a slow speed. For any turning operation, hold the tool so its bevel is rubbing against the wood, then pivot it up to engage the cutting edge.

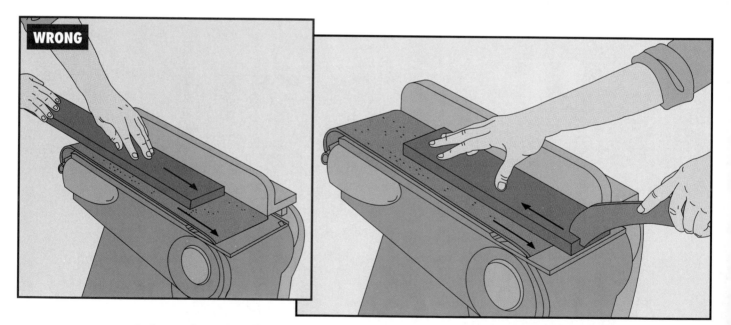

Belt-sander catapult.

If you feed a board onto the belt in the same direction as its rotation *(above, left)*, the sander can rip the board out of your hands and launch it at great speed, exposing your hands to the spinning sandpaper. Instead, feed the wood against the direction of the belt's rotation and protect the hand pushing the work from the belt by using a push stick *(above, right)*.

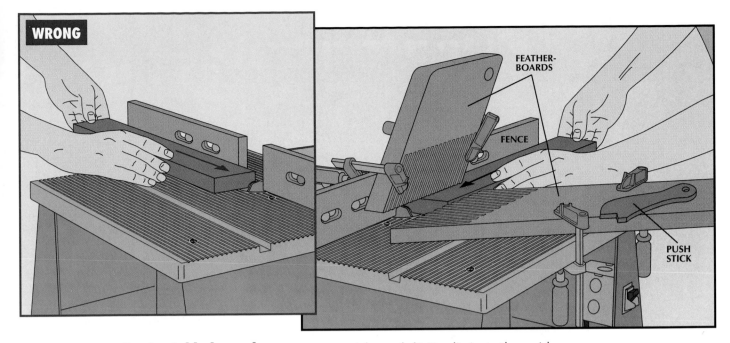

Router-table hazards.

If the workpiece is not kept against the table and fence, the bit can grab it and throw it back at you. If you feed the wood into the bit in its direction of rotation, the wood—and your hand—may be pulled toward the bit *(above, left)*. To eliminate these risks, clamp a pair of featherboards *(page 90)* to the fence and table. Feed the wood into the bit against the bit's direction of rotation *(above, right)*, and guide the end of the piece past the bit with a push stick.

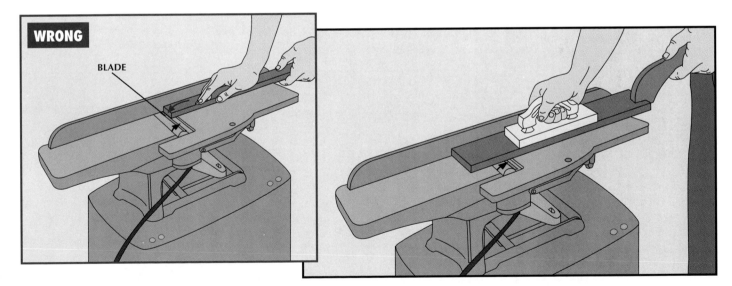

Jointer jump.

When smoothing a board face on the jointer—known as face-jointing—the blades of the tool can grab the end of a small or improperly guided board and pull it—and possibly your hand—into the machine *(above, left)*. Avoid jointer jump by face-jointing wood no thinner than $\frac{1}{2}$ inch and no less than 12 inches long. Set the depth of cut to a maximum of $\frac{1}{16}$ inch to help prevent kickback. Always use the spring guard over the blades; it has been omitted here for the sake of clarity. Keep the wood flat against the table with a push block, and distance your fingers from the blades with a push stick *(above, right)*.

Laying Out the Shop

Whatever the shape and size of a workshop—or how special its purpose—it should be arranged to conserve space and motion. Group tools according to function, with nearby storage for accessories. Make electricity available where it is needed, for both light and power.

Planning on Paper: Begin your layout with a floor plan of the existing space drawn to scale on standard graph paper. Note the locations of windows, doors, stairs, supporting columns, and other permanent architectural features. Include anything that intrudes on the shop space—a furnace, water heater, freezer, washer, or dryer. If the shop is in the garage, indicate the space occupied by the car.

Make paper cutouts, also drawn to scale, of the benches, cabinets, and power tools you intend to install, and move them around on the layout until you find a satisfactory arrangement. Try arranging tools in the sequence in which they will be used. In a woodworking shop, for example, cutting and shaping tools (a saw, a jointer, and a lathe) should lead to assembly (a drill press), then to finishing (a sander). Allow for sufficient work space and auxiliary work surfaces around each tool. Position the workbench and lathe near windows, if possible, to benefit from natural light, and place power tools near electrical outlets. You will need shadow-free light overhead for a table saw, sander, or jointer; but a drill press, band saw, or scroll saw can go into a corner with less light, since you can equip these tools with a lamp.

Finding More Room: There are several ways to make your available area work for you. To conserve space, you can buy a radial-arm saw, which fits against a wall, rather than a table saw, which requires 10 feet of space all around. Or, you can build a fold-down workbench that stores out of the way when it is not needed *(page 77)*. Save room by mounting bulky tools on roll-away stands that can be pushed into a corner or under a table when not in use. You may decide to forgo stationary power tools altogether, opting for portable ones that can be fastened to a tabletop to do a comparable job. What you lose in performance will save both money and space.

PLOTTING A TRAFFIC PATTERN

Laying out a step-saving circle.
In a spacious, well-equipped shop *(right)*, tools and work surfaces are arranged in a circle that reflects the natural flow of a typical woodworking project. Storage is located near the table saw, jointer, and lathe, which are commonly used at the start of a job. A band saw and a scroll saw for shaping are lined up along the wall with a drill press.

Nearby stands a worktable for assembly. The shop's main workbench is positioned between two windows, to make optimum use of natural light.

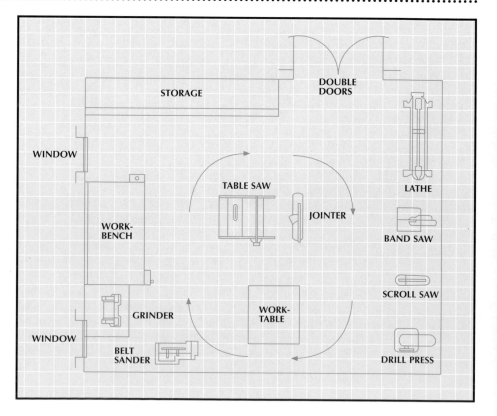

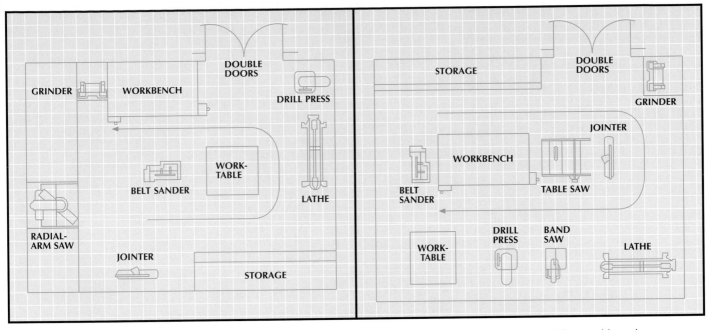

Fitting a shop in small spaces.
To make the best use of a smaller space, set up your shop so work flows in a U—from storage to cutting and shaping to assembly and finally to finishing. One option is to buy a radial-arm saw *(above, left),* which can be positioned against a wall, freeing the center of the shop for finishing tasks. Another is to build the shop around a central island formed by the workbench, a table saw, and a jointer *(above, right).* This arrangement allows both sides of the workbench to be used. If your shop has double doors, they can be left open to provide space when you are working long boards on the saw or jointer.

TRICKS OF THE TRADE

Squeezing Stationary Machines into Confined Spaces

Even if your shop is cramped, you need not forgo large power tools. Consider the design of the machines and their feed directions—you may be able to place two machines quite close together if they are well matched. With a band saw and a jointer, for example, the jointer can be located next to the outfeed end of the saw's relatively high worktable *(right).* The two tools will not interfere with each other, and the jointer fence can even serve as an auxiliary table for the saw.

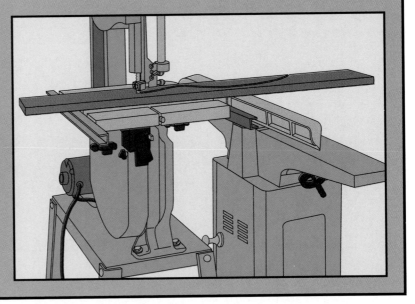

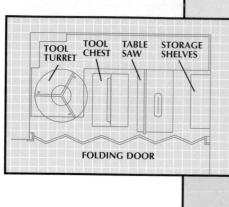

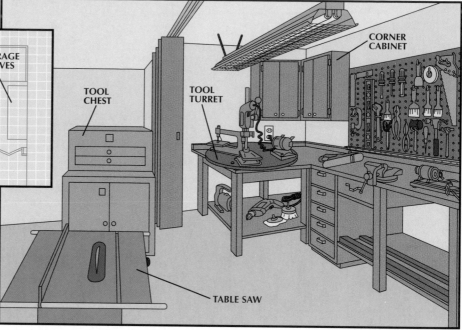

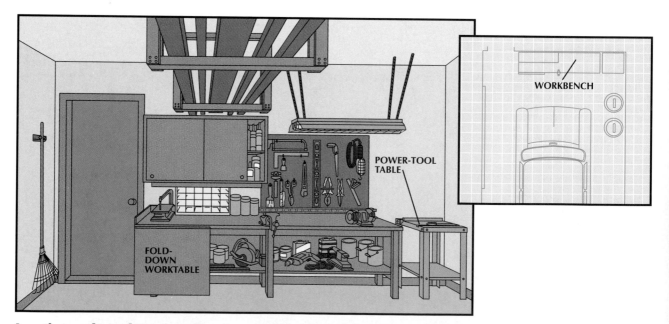

Setting up an expandable shop.

Fitted into an alcove behind folding doors when not in use *(inset)*, a shop can share space with a recreation room, den, or garage. Large items such as the tool chest and the table saw are mounted on locking casters and can be rolled into posi-

tion *(above)*. The L-shaped workbench—two rectangular benches joined by a single top—is large enough to accommodate a vise, a small lathe, and a revolving tool turret *(page 103)*. This one features a scroll saw, a drill stand, and a grinder.

Locating a shop along a wall.

Set at the end of a garage *(inset)*, the shop illustrated above is built around a workbench that covers most of the wall. The bench expands to an L-shaped surface when the hinged table on the

left side is raised. Overhead racks suspended from the ceiling provide storage space for lumber. A commercial power-tool table can accommodate a circular saw or router—becoming a small table saw or router table.

A Shop Dolly

A wheeled dolly is a convenient way to move tools and projects around, particularly in a compact shop. Cut the base and corner blocks from $\frac{3}{4}$-inch plywood. Screw the blocks to the plywood and fasten a caster to each block. Cut the eight skirt pieces and the eight leg pieces from 1-by-3 stock, the shelf from $\frac{1}{2}$-inch plywood, and the top from $\frac{3}{4}$-inch plywood. Glue the leg pieces together, fastening them with $1\frac{1}{2}$-inch No. 6 screws, then screw the skirts to the inside face of the legs. Fasten the shelf and the top to the skirts, then secure the legs to the base with angle irons.

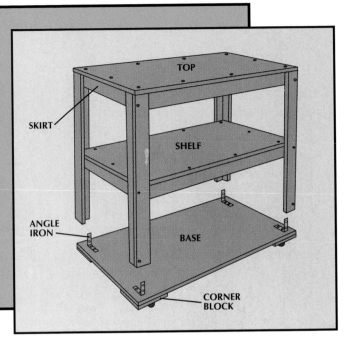

Hiding a shop in a closet.

A closet shop is more than just a convenient place to store tools. Replace a hollow-core door with a solid one, then attach a small fold-down work surface made of $\frac{3}{4}$-inch plywood to the inside of the door, supporting it with heavy-duty folding brackets. To extend the work surface, mount a shelf at the same height inside the closet on 2-by-4s nailed to the studs in the closet walls. A clamp-on work lamp provides light. A tool caddy (page 94) on the floor holds hand tools, while power tools are stored in a wheeled chest. Equipped with locking casters, the chest can serve as a work surface. The holders at the bottom of the door keep the door from moving when the work surface is being used.

A shop needs two circuits, one for power tools and another for lighting.

Tapping Into Existing Circuits:
If there already are two circuits in the shop, you may be able to add lighting and new outlets for portable power tools. If not, extending one or more circuits in adjoining locations may work *(below and opposite)*.

Choose circuits not controlled by switches. To determine whether a circuit has enough spare capacity, add up the wattages of all the devices that are likely to be drawing power from it at the same time. Divide the total by the number of volts carried by the circuit—either 120 or 240—to obtain the amps drawn, then subtract this amount from the amperage rating of the circuit. If the result is 10 or more amps, the circuit has enough spare capacity to run most tools.

Avoid tapping into existing circuits if your house wiring is aluminum or if you'll be powering stationary tools. Additional circuits are called for.

New Circuits: Stationary power tools or an electric heater each require a dedicated circuit. Such circuits can originate from a 40-amp circuit breaker in the main panel, extend to an auxiliary panel called a subpanel with No. 8 cable, and branch off individually from the subpanel. Although you can install the subpanel and do the circuit wiring yourself *(pages 51-57)*, have an electrician connect the new circuit to the service panel.

Before you start wiring, check local electrical code requirements. For example, be sure to match each circuit's wire size to the capacity of its circuit breaker or fuse. For 15-amp lighting circuits, use No. 14 copper wire; for 20-amp circuits, use No. 12 wire.

Reduce the chance of shock by installing ground-fault circuit interrupters (GFCIs), either in the form of a circuit breaker or a receptacle. Designed to detect minuscule current leaks and cut off the circuit in $\frac{1}{40}$ second, GFCI protection is required for 120-volt 15- and 20-amp circuits serving workbenches.

TOOLS

Voltage tester	Masonry bit
Cable ripper	Maul
Wire stripper	Star drill
Punch	Extension bits
Hammer	Putty knife
Electric drill	Electrician's fish tape
	Screwdriver

MATERIALS

Electrical cable	Plastic pipe
Cable clamps	Latex concrete-patching compound
Wire caps	Cable straps
GFCI outlet	Screw anchors and screws
Surface electrical box ($3\frac{1}{2}$")	Light chain
Jumper wires	Electrician's tape
Common nails ($2\frac{1}{4}$")	Sealing putty
1 x 2s	Plywood ($3\frac{1}{4}$")
Cable staples	Circuit breakers

SAFETY TIPS

Wear goggles when operating power tools, nailing, or chiseling masonry.

EXTENDING EXISTING CIRCUITS

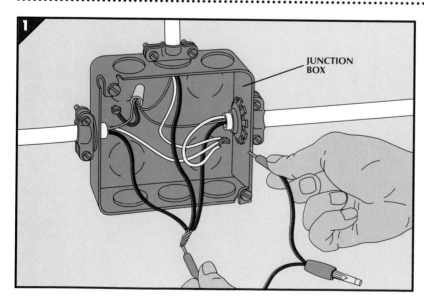

JUNCTION BOX

1. Locating a cable for tapping.

◆ Find a junction box on a circuit with extra capacity.

◆ Trip all the circuit breakers in the service panel and open the junction box. Remove wire caps and check all pairs of wires and grounds with a voltage tester *(left)*, which will not glow if all the power is off.

◆ To identify the circuit at the service panel, have a helper turn on the circuit breakers one at a time until the voltage tester glows. Then have your helper operate any switches on the circuit. If the tester continues to glow, the circuit is suitable for tapping.

◆ Trip the circuit breaker for this circuit, then turn on all the other circuit breakers, restoring power to the rest of the house.

2. Adding a new cable.

◆ Remove a knockout from the junction box with a punch and hammer and secure a cable clamp to the box.

◆ Strip 6 inches of sheathing from one end of a cable, strip $\frac{3}{4}$ inch of insulation from the end of each cable wire, then feed the cable through the cable clamp and tighten it.

◆ With wire caps, connect the cable's bare copper wire to the other bare copper ground wires and the green ground jumper wire.

◆ Connect the cable's white neutral wire to the white wires and its black wire to the black wires *(right)*.

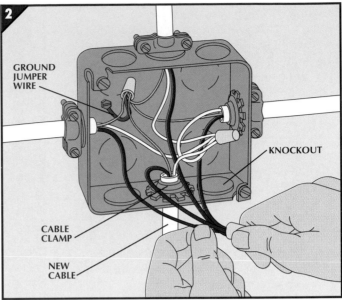

GROUND JUMPER WIRE

KNOCKOUT

CABLE CLAMP

NEW CABLE

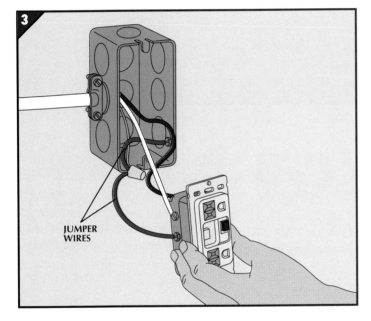

JUMPER WIRES

3. Wiring a GFCI receptacle.

◆ To install a surface-style GFCI outlet at the workshop end of the new cable, fasten a $3\frac{1}{2}$-inch-deep surface box to the wall. Remove a knockout hole on one side and secure a cable clamp. Strip the new cable, slide it into the box and fasten it with the cable clamp.

◆ Attach the white wire to the terminal screw marked LINE WHITE. Attach the black wire to the terminal screw marked LINE BLACK.

◆ Attach one green jumper wire to the terminal screw marked GROUND and another to the box. With wire caps, connect the cable's bare copper wire to the green jumper wires.

◆ Screw the GFCI and an outlet cover to the box.

PATHWAYS FOR WIRES

Crossing the house.

To extend electrical cable to the shop from a location in another part of the house, use the framing members of an unfinished basement, crawl space, or attic as pathways. In a basement, you may be able to use a girder or the edge of a sill plate as a route *(right)*. To run cable across joists, fasten 1-by-2s perpendicular to the joists along the cable route to protect the cable from being snagged. Secure the cable with cable staples every 4 feet and within 1 foot of each cable end.

Passing through concrete block.

◆ With a masonry bit, drill a hole through the block for the cable. You are most likely to pierce through the hollow spaces in the block if you place the hole 3 inches from the end of the block and center it between the top and bottom.

◆ With a star drill and a maul *(right)*, enlarge the hole to about 2 inches in diameter to accommodate a length of $1\frac{1}{4}$-inch-inside-diameter conduit, which will house the cable and cable clamp.

◆ Trim the conduit so it spans the opening and insert it into the hole. Plug the gap around the conduit with latex concrete-patching compound.

To run cable along a concrete-block wall, thread it through metal cable conduit secured to the block at 4-foot intervals with cable straps held by screws and plastic screw anchors.

⚠️ **CAUTION** *Metal conduit must be grounded. Normally this requirement is met when it is secured to the subpanel or any grounded electrical box.*

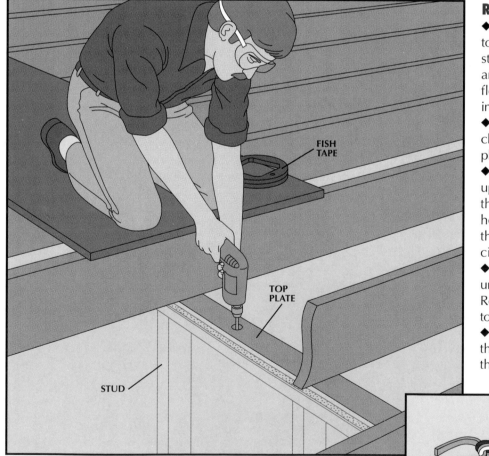

FISH TAPE

TOP PLATE

STUD

Running cable within a wall.

◆ In the attic, drill a hole through the top plate into the space between two studs *(left)*. Then go to the basement and drill a hole up through the ground floor's sole plate in line with the hole in the attic.

◆ Have a helper in the attic drop a light chain down through the hole in the top plate to the sole plate.

◆ From the basement, push a fish tape up through the sole plate hole, catch the chain, and pull it down through the hole. Secure the chain to the hook at the end of the fish tape with electrician's tape.

◆ Have your helper pull the chain up until the fish tape reaches the attic. Remove the chain and attach the cable to the tape hook *(inset)*.

◆ Pull the fish tape down until the end of the cable emerges from the sole plate.

ALL-PURPOSE WIRING LAYOUT

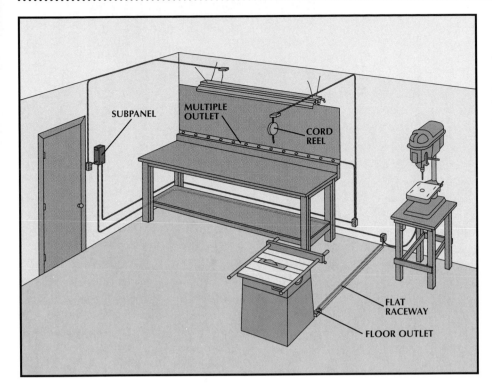

SUBPANEL

MULTIPLE OUTLET

CORD REEL

FLAT RACEWAY

FLOOR OUTLET

Laying out the cable and outlets.

In the shop illustrated at left, three separate circuits stem from a subpanel near the door. One feeds a switched circuit to a fluorescent light above the workbench. Another serves a string of outlets along the back of the bench for portable power tools; an overhead outlet on a cord reel; and a standard wall outlet. A third circuit powers outlets located near stationary tools, including a floor outlet for the table saw. All cables are encased in steel conduit or raceway.

The circuit breakers for the bench outlets and the stationary tools can be shut off and the subpanel locked to prevent unauthorized use.

INSTALLING A SUBPANEL

1. Clamping the new cable.

◆ Run No. 8 three-conductor-with-ground cable from the service panel to the subpanel location. Leave 5 feet of extra cable at the service-panel end and 2 extra feet at the subpanel end.
◆ For a cable entering the subpanel from the side, first mount the subpanel *(Step 2)*, then clamp the cable and strip its sheathing.

◆ If the cable will enter the back of the subpanel, first thread a cable clamp over the cable, pack putty into the pipe around the cable, and slide the clamp to the wall, leaving a 2-foot end *(right)*.
◆ Tighten the clamp's screws to secure the cable, then push the gripping portion of the clamp into the pipe. Pack putty around the cable at the other end of the pipe.
◆ Strip the cable sheathing back to the clamp.

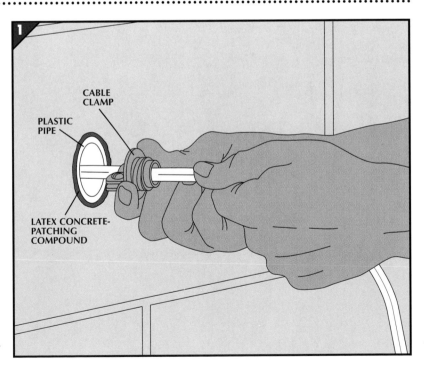

CABLE CLAMP

PLASTIC PIPE

LATEX CONCRETE-PATCHING COMPOUND

2. Mounting the subpanel.

◆ If the cable is to enter from the rear, thread it temporarily through the hole in the box so the subpanel can fit flush against the wall. With a helper holding the subpanel against the wall, mark its mounting holes.

◆ Remove the subpanel from the wall and drill a hole at each mark. Insert lead or plastic screw anchors into the holes.

◆ Thread the cable through the subpanel box and, with the cable clamp against the back of the box, mount it by driving screws into the screw anchors *(right)*.

If the wall is likely to be damp, as in basements, mount a piece of $\frac{3}{4}$-inch plywood to the wall and secure the subpanel to it.

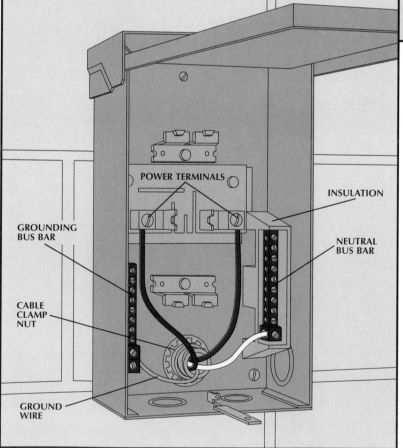

POWER TERMINALS

INSULATION

GROUNDING BUS BAR

NEUTRAL BUS BAR

CABLE CLAMP NUT

GROUND WIRE

3. Connecting the wires.

◆ Put the cable clamp nut on the clamp and tighten it against the box.

◆ Separate the four cable wires and strip $\frac{1}{2}$ inch of insulation off their ends.

◆ Connect the four wires as follows: the bare ground wire to a large terminal on the uninsulated grounding bus bar, the white neutral wire to the large terminal on the insulated neutral bus bar, the black wire to one power terminal, and the red wire to the other power terminal.

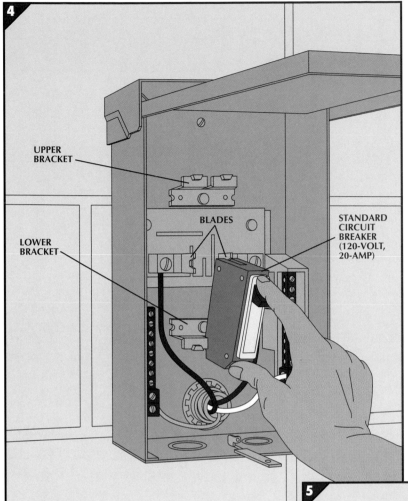

UPPER BRACKET

BLADES

LOWER BRACKET

STANDARD CIRCUIT BREAKER (120-VOLT, 20-AMP)

4. Installing a circuit breaker.

Snap a circuit breaker designed for your subpanel onto its holder in the box. To install a standard 120-volt, 20-amp breaker, suitable for a lighting circuit, in the model shown, first slip the breaker onto the lower bracket *(left)*, then press it onto the blade connected to one 120-volt power terminal.

A 240-volt breaker would engage the two upper brackets and two blades, side by side; with each blade connected to a separate 120-volt terminal, the total capacity of the breaker would be 240 volts.

5. Wiring a GFCI breaker.

◆ Snap a 120- or 240-volt GFCI breaker into place as in Step 4.
◆ Uncoil the breaker's white neutral wire and lead it to the insulated neutral bus bar of the subpanel.
◆ Cut the wire to fit and strip off $\frac{1}{2}$ inch of insulation.
◆ Fasten the wire to a free terminal on the neutral bus bar *(right)*.

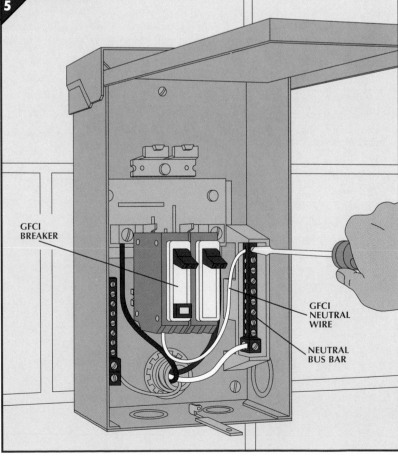

GFCI BREAKER

GFCI NEUTRAL WIRE

NEUTRAL BUS BAR

Once you have brought electrical power to the shop, you must then distribute it to outlets.

Wiring: New circuits from a sub-panel or the main service panel can be either 120 or 240 volts *(below and pages 55-57)*. Tools such as arc welders and certain stationary saws require a 240-volt circuit. Check electrical code requirements in your area, and when the electrician comes to hook up any new installations to the electrical service, have all your new wiring checked.

Outlets: A common duplex receptacle in a surface-mounted box *(page 56)* can power a tool placed along a wall. Multi-outlet strips above a workbench are also convenient *(page 58)*. Another option is to hang an extension-cord reel from the ceiling *(page 59)*. If you buy a reconditioned stationary tool without a built-in switch, you can install a lockable switch on it for safety and convenience *(pages 60-61)*.

Guarding Cables: Protect the wires to outlets with plastic or metal conduit or raceway. Thin-walled metal conduit (EMT) costs more than plastic tubes, which must be joined with cemented plastic fittings. The neatest but costliest option is rectangular metal raceway. Where the wiring needs to be flexible, as seen on page 61, armored cable offers security and is easy to install.

⚠️ **CAUTION** *Metal conduit must be grounded. Normally this requirement is met when it is secured to the subpanel or any grounded electrical box.*

 TOOLS

Carpenter's level
Ball-peen hammer
Punch
Hacksaw
Round file
Screwdriver
Cable ripper
Wire strippers
Electric drill
Masonry bit

 MATERIALS

Electrical conduit
Conduit connectors
Corner elbows
Conduit straps
Electric cable
Cable clamps
Screw anchors and screws
Receptacles
Jumper wires (green and black)
Wire caps
Outlet boxes
Circuit breakers
Multi-outlet strip
Floor raceway kit
Extension-cord reel
Screw hook
Switch box and safety plate
Electrical cord
Plug
Armored cable, bushings, and clamps
Junction box

 **SAFETY TIPS**

Wear goggles when drilling into masonry.

CARRYING A CIRCUIT WITH CONDUIT

1. Laying out the conduit path.

◆ Mark the locations of the outlets and junction boxes, then fasten them to the wall just as you secured the subpanel *(page 52, Step 2)*.
◆ Choose a knockout opening in the subpanel at an appropriate location for the circuit you are running. With a level, mark vertical and horizontal lines on the wall to trace the conduit path from the subpanel *(right)*.
◆ Remove the knockout from the subpanel with a hammer and punch. Insert a conduit connector in the hole and secure the connector with its retaining nut. You may need to employ an offset connector to bring the conduit against the wall *(inset)*.

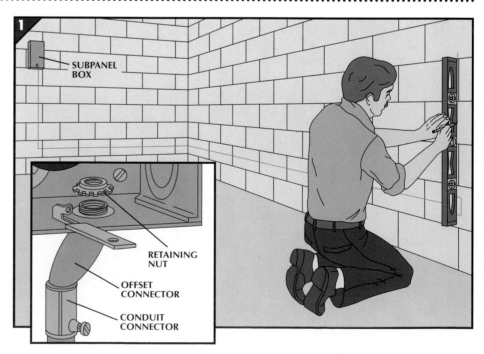

SUBPANEL BOX

RETAINING NUT

OFFSET CONNECTOR

CONDUIT CONNECTOR

OFFSET CONNECTOR

CORNER ELBOW

2. Cutting conduit.

◆ Mark a length of conduit to span between the subpanel and first run of horizontal conduit. Cut the conduit with a hacksaw and ream the inside rim with a round file to remove burrs, which can cut into cable.

◆ Secure one end to the connector at the subpanel and add a corner elbow to the other end.

◆ Place the first horizontal piece in position, in this case leaving space for an elbow in the corner. Mark the piece where it crosses the vertical section *(above)*, then cut it to length and attach it to the elbow.

◆ Continue to mark, cut, and add sections along the marked path to the next outlet location. Secure the conduit to the outlet box with a conduit connector. Install remaining conduit and boxes in the same manner.

3. Running cable.

◆ Disassemble all the fittings at their joints to facilitate running the cable through the conduit.

◆ Starting at the elbow nearest the middle of the run and working toward the ends, push two-conductor-with-ground cable through the conduit and fittings into the boxes at either end. Pull the cable taut *(right)*, leaving about 8 inches of cable protruding from each box and at the subpanel, and cut it.

◆ Reassemble the conduit joints.

◆ To fasten the conduit to the wall, drill holes for screw anchors, then screw in straps, placing them 4 feet apart and within 1 foot of each end.

◆ Strip the cable sheathing back to the conduit connector.

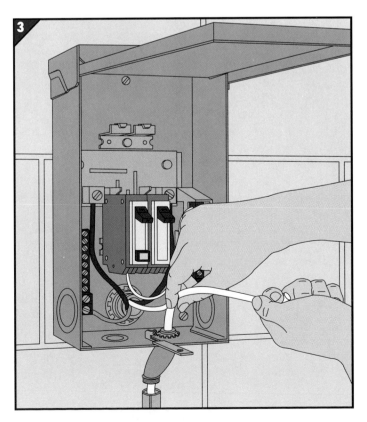

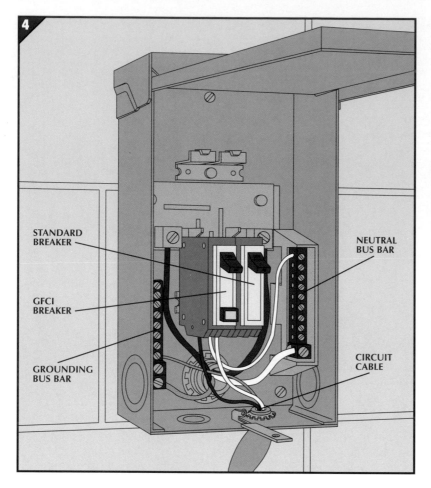

4

STANDARD
BREAKER

GFCI
BREAKER

GROUNDING
BUS BAR

NEUTRAL
BUS BAR

CIRCUIT
CABLE

4. Hooking up the cable.

◆ Connect the bare ground wire of the circuit cable to the subpanel's grounding bus bar.

◆ Prepare the other wires by stripping $\frac{1}{2}$ inch of insulation from them.

◆ To wire a GFCI breaker, connect the white neutral wire to the terminal on the breaker marked with a white dot and labeled LOAD NEUTRAL. Connect the black wire to the terminal labeled LOAD.

◆ For a standard 120-volt breaker, attach the neutral wire of the cable to the neutral bus bar and the black wire to the circuit breaker terminal.

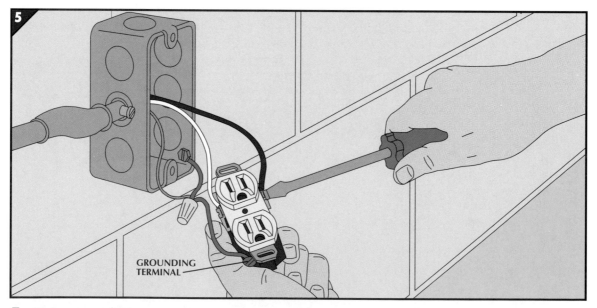

5

GROUNDING
TERMINAL

5. Wiring an outlet.

◆ Strip the cable wire ends.

◆ Attach one green jumper wire to a screw terminal on the wall of the box and another to the green grounding terminal of the receptacle. With a wire cap, join both jumpers with the cable's bare wire.

◆ Connect the white cable wire to a silver ter-

minal of the receptacle and the black wire to a brass terminal *(above)*.

◆ To extend the wiring to another outlet, install conduit in another knockout, then connect the cable's bare wire to the green wires. Attach the cable's white wire to the remaining silver terminal on the receptacle, and the black wire to the brass terminal.

WIRING A 240-VOLT CIRCUIT

Connecting a 240-volt circuit breaker.

A 240-volt circuit can usually be wired with two-conductor-with-ground cable as shown here. High-wattage appliances such as kilns require a three-conductor-with-ground cable; its neutral conductor is attached to the neutral bus bar. Before wiring a circuit for a shop machine, check the owner's manual for electrical requirements.

◆ Run conduit and cable to the subpanel box *(pages 54-55, Steps 1-3)*.

◆ Snap a 240-volt circuit breaker designed for the subpanel box into position *(page 53, Step 4)*.

◆ Paint the end of the white wire black to indicate that it will be live, and not neutral.

◆ Wire the breaker by connecting the bare cable wire to the grounding bus bar, and the white and black wires to separate breaker terminals *(right)*.

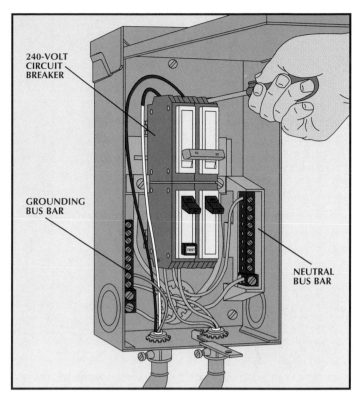

240-VOLT CIRCUIT BREAKER

GROUNDING BUS BAR

NEUTRAL BUS BAR

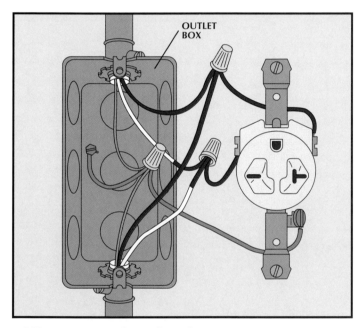

OUTLET BOX

Adding a 240-volt outlet along a run.

◆ Attach short lengths of green jumper wire to the green grounding screws of the receptacle and the outlet box.

◆ Attach short black jumper wires to each of the remaining terminals on the receptacle. (The receptacle can be oriented with the grounding slot up or down.)

◆ Paint the ends of the white wires black to indicate that they will be live.

◆ With a wire cap, join the bare wires from the two cables and the two green jumper wires. Connect the two black cable wires to one of the black jumper wires on the receptacle, and the white cable wires to the other black jumper wire.

◆ Screw the receptacle in place and attach a cover.

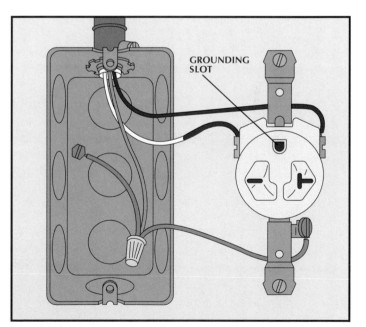

GROUNDING SLOT

A 240-volt outlet at the end of a run.

◆ Fasten short green jumper wires to the green grounding screws of the receptacle and outlet box.

◆ With a wire cap, connect the cable's bare ground wire to the green jumper wires.

◆ Paint the end of the white wire black to indicate that it will be live.

◆ Fasten the black cable wire to the brass terminal screw on the receptacle, and the white wire to the silver screw.

OUTLETS THAT BRING POWER TO THE JOB

Mounting a multi-outlet strip.

◆ Screw the base of a multi-outlet strip to the wall so the small junction box is at the end where power will enter *(right)*, and run conduit and cable to it. For portable power tools, consider mounting the strip on the front of the bench to keep the cords out of the way.

◆ With wire caps, connect the bare cable wire to the green wire of the outlet strip; the white cable wire to the white outlet wire; and the black cable wire to the black outlet wire.

◆ At the other end of the strip, connect the green wire to the grounding clip that clamps into the outlet-strip base. Cover exposed wire ends with wire caps.

◆ Snap the outlet strip onto the base.

A power bar with an internal circuit breaker *(photograph)* is a simpler version of a multi-outlet strip.

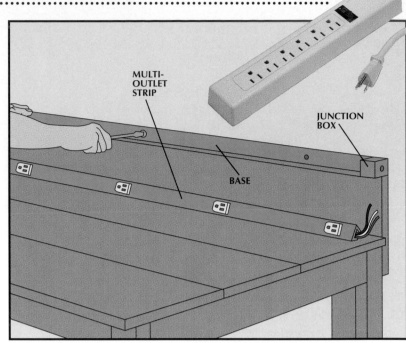

Wiring a floor outlet.

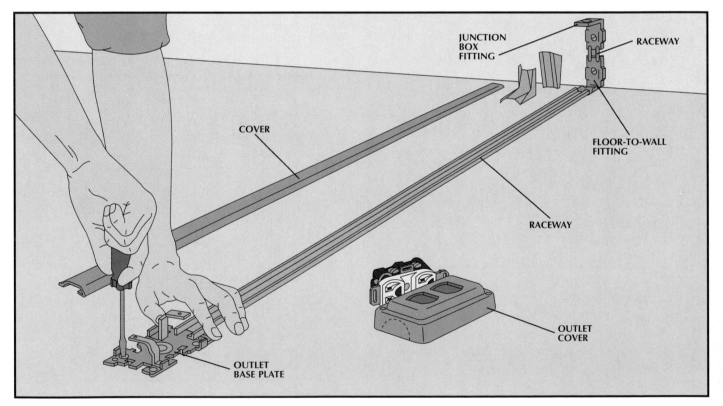

◆ Place the base plate of a raceway floor outlet box in the desired location, then lay out prescored raceway and fittings on the floor.

◆ Snap off the raceway to the correct length, or cut it with a hacksaw. Cut each cover section $\frac{3}{4}$ inch shorter than the corresponding length of raceway.

◆ Drill holes in the floor for screw anchors, then fasten the raceway and base plate to the floor *(above)*.

◆ Lay cable inside the raceway and connect it to the receptacle *(page 56, Step 5)*.

◆ Fasten the receptacle to the base plate and snap the cover sections over the raceway. Attach the outlet cover, twisting out the scored semicircle to fit it over the raceway.

◆ To complete the circuit, run cable in conduit from the subpanel to the junction-box fitting. Add a junction box, then connect the two cables. Finally, cover the floor-to-wall and junction-box fittings.

EXTENSION-
CORD REEL

Hanging an extension-cord reel.

An extension-cord reel can neatly store heavy-duty cords 50 feet or longer.

◆ Drive a screw hook into a joist at a convenient point and hang a cord reel from it.

◆ Install an outlet box on the joist within reach of the cord-reel plug and run conduit and cable from the box to a source of power.

◆ Connect the cable to the outlet and mount it in the box.

◆ Put the cover on the outlet box and plug in the cord reel.

TRICKS OF THE TRADE

A Power-Cord Cover

Power cords lying across the floor are both an electrical and a tripping hazard. While raceway is most suitable for a permanent installation, other solutions are available. For example, you can temporarily secure a cord to the floor with duct tape. A more permanent alternative is to buy a rubber cord protector—or you can make a wooden one in your shop from a 1-by-3 *(right)*.

Cut the board to length, then use a router to groove one face of the board for the cord. Bevel the other face so that the cord protector presents less of an obstacle.

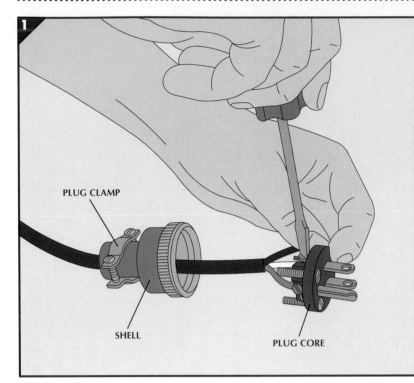

1. Attaching the plug.

◆ Mount a switch box in a convenient location on the tool stand.

◆ Cut a length of Type SJ three-wire flexible cord, sized in accordance with the tool's current rating, to reach from the outlet to the switch box.

◆ Loosen the screws on the face of the plug to separate the plug core and shell.

◆ Slip the shell over the cord, then remove $1\frac{1}{2}$ inches of sheathing to expose the three wires.

◆ Strip $\frac{3}{4}$ inch of insulation from each wire end and connect the wires to the plug terminal screws—black wire to the brass screw *(left)*, white wire to the silver screw, and green wire to the green screw.

◆ Reassemble the plug and secure it with the faceplate screws. Tighten the plug clamp.

2. Wiring a switch to the cord.

◆ With a hammer and punch, remove a knockout from a switch box.

◆ Secure a cable clamp to the box, strip 6 inches of sheathing from the end of the cord, and thread it through the knockout hole in the box; tighten the clamp around it.

◆ Attach short lengths of green jumper wire to the green grounding screws of the switch and outlet box.

◆ With a wire cap, join the cord's green wire and the two green jumper wires. Attach the black wire to one of the terminal screws on the side of the switch *(right)*; do not attach the white wire yet.

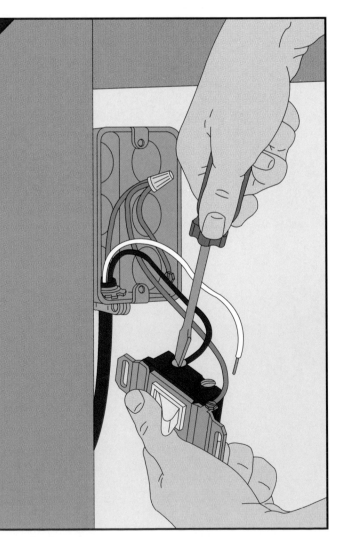

3. Connecting the motor.

◆ With a hacksaw, cut a length of armored cable to fit between the switch box and the tool's junction box.

◆ Remove 4 inches of the armor from the cable at each end. To do so: Cut perpendicular to the direction of the spirals, then break off the armor.

◆ Insert a protective bushing into each end of the cable armor *(right)*; wrap the thin bond wire back around the cable armor to secure the bushing.

◆ Fasten the cable to the motor with cable clamps designed for armored cable.

◆ Connect the wires at the motor as indicated on the manufacturer's specification plate or on the diagram in the junction box.

◆ At the switch box, fasten the cable with cable clamps designed for armored cable. Connect the white cable wire to the white wire of the flexible cord, and the black cable wire to the remaining screw terminal of the switch.

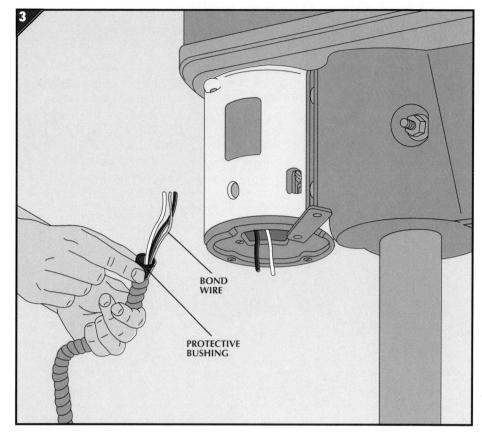

BOND WIRE

PROTECTIVE BUSHING

FLANGE

4. A flanged switch plate.

On the box, mount a switch cover-plate equipped with safety flanges drilled for a padlock. The flanges help prevent clothing from accidentally tripping the switch. A lock through the holes guards against unauthorized use of the tool.

Workshops need two kinds of light: general overhead lighting and light aimed directly on the work at hand. The first need is met by permanent fixtures; the second is best served by a portable plug-in fixture.

Fluorescent Lighting: An ideal fluorescent fixture for the shop consists of two 40-watt tubes 4 feet long mounted in a metal box incorporating a reflector, a ballast transformer, wiring, and four lamp holders. The lighting unit can be mounted directly to a low ceiling, or hung on chains where a ceiling is higher.

Switches: Fixtures can be controlled by switches mounted directly on the units, by wall switches, or by both. Wall switches for overhead lights are wired in one of two ways. In middle-of-the-line wiring, the switch is placed between the power source and the light fixture and the power goes from source to fixture in a direct line (below and opposite). A fixture that lies between the source and the switch is wired with a switch loop—the power goes first to the fixture outlet box, where it is diverted to the switch and back to the fixture via the same cable (pages 64-65). If you are wiring two or more lights in a circuit controlled by one end-of-line switch (pages 65-66), run three-conductor-with-ground cable between the fixtures.

Portable Light: Lamps that direct light where it is needed come in both incandescent and fluorescent designs. The extension-arm light (page 67) clamps onto almost any bench and has a mounting shaft that can be fitted into a hole drilled in the workbench or a tool stand, so the fixture can be moved quickly from one spot to another.

 TOOLS

Ball-peen hammer
Punch
Cable ripper
Wire strippers

Diagonal-cutting
   pliers
Screwdriver
Electric drill
Masonry bit
Carpenter's level

 **MATERIALS**

Electrical cord
Cable clamps
Wire caps
Fluorescent light
   fixture
Pull-chain switch
Lightweight chain
S-hooks
Screw eyes

Outlet boxes
Conduit and
   fittings
Electrical cable
Green jumper
   wire
Light switch
2 x 2
Screw anchors
Wood screws
   (3" No. 8)

SAFETY TIPS

When working overhead or when drilling or nailing, protect your eyes with goggles.

HANGING A SWITCHED FLUORESCENT FIXTURE

1. Wiring the fixture.

◆ Strip 6 inches of sheathing from one end of a spool of Type SJ No. 16 three-wire flexible cord; strip the wire ends. Secure a cable clamp to the box, slide the cord through a knockout hole in the fixture, and fasten it with the clamp.

◆ Secure the cord's green wire to the grounding screw of the box.

◆ With wire caps, join the white cord wire to the white fixture wire and, unless you are adding a switch to the fixture (Step 2), connect the black cord wire to the black fixture wire (right).

◆ Assemble the rest of the fixture following the manufacturer's instructions.

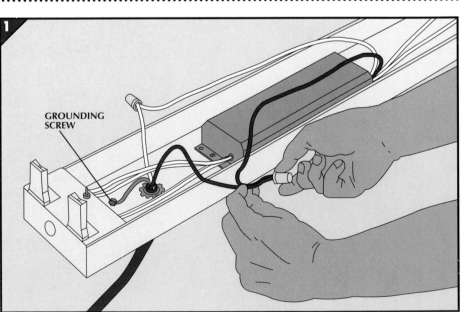

GROUNDING
SCREW

2. Adding a switch to the fixture.

◆ To control the light with a pull-chain switch mounted on the fixture, fasten the black cord wire to one of the switch wires. Fasten the other switch wire to the black fixture wire.

◆ Insert the switch into a knockout hole in the fixture's end plate and secure the switch with its retaining nut.

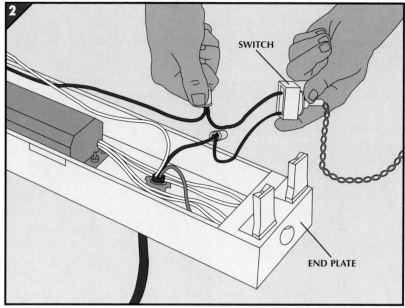

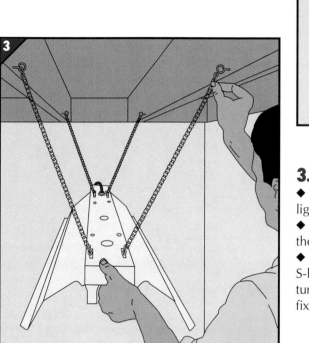

3. Hanging the fixture.

◆ With diagonal-cutting pliers cut four equal lengths of lightweight chain to hang the fixture at the desired height.

◆ Attach one chain to each of the openings in the top of the fixture with S-hooks.

◆ Twist screw eyes into the joists above the work area. Slip S-hooks into the free end of each chain and hang the fixture from the screw eyes (left). To adjust the height of the fixture, reposition the chain links on the upper S-hooks.

4. Running power to the fixture.

◆ Install an outlet box for the light switch and another one near the fixture. Run conduit and No. 14 two-conductor-with-ground cable from the main service panel or a subpanel to the switch box, then continue with another cable to the fixture box (pages 54-56).

◆ Fasten a length of green jumper wire to the green grounding screws in both boxes and to the switch.

◆ At the switch box, connect the bare wires of the two cables to the green jumper wires with wire caps. Connect the white wires of the cables together, and the two black cable wires to separate switch terminals.

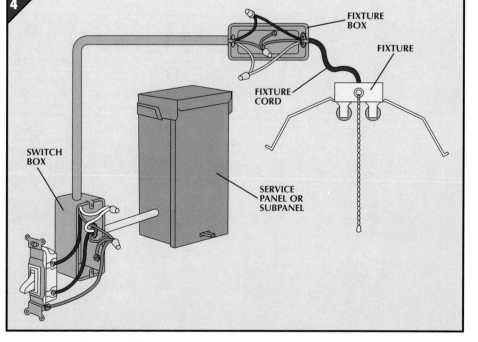

◆ At the fixture box, join the green jumper wire, the bare cable wire, and the green cord wire with a wire cap.

Connect the white cable wire to the white cord wire and the black cable wire to the black cord wire.

WIRING AN END-OF-LINE SWITCH

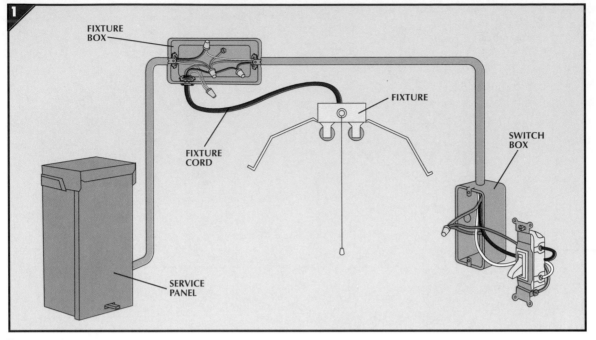

1. Planning the circuit.

The diagram above shows the wiring layout for a fixture box with a light switch. In an end-of-line circuit (above), cable is first run from the service panel to the fixture box. The fixture is wired to the box and another run of cable extends to the switch box.

◆ Run conduit and No. 14 two-conductor-with-ground cable from the service panel or subpanel to a fixture box near the light fixture; run a second cable with conduit from the box to another box at the light-switch location (pages 54-56).

◆ Wire the light fixture with Type SJ No. 16 three-wire flexible cord (page 62, Step 1) and clamp the fixture cord to the fixture box.

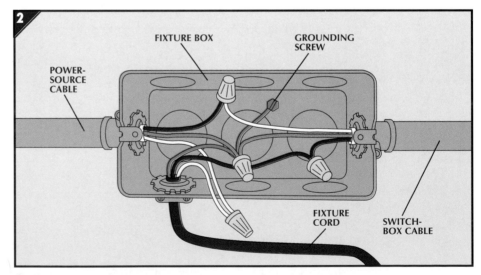

2. Wiring the fixture box.

◆ Fasten a green jumper wire to the grounding screw of the fixture box.

◆ With a wire cap, connect the bare wires of the two cables to the green wire of the fixture cord and the green jumper wire.

◆ Connect the white wire of the power-source cable to the fixture cord's white wire.

◆ Join the black wire of the power-source cable to the white wire of the cable going to the switch box.

◆ Connect the black wire of the switch-box cable to the black wire of the fixture cord.

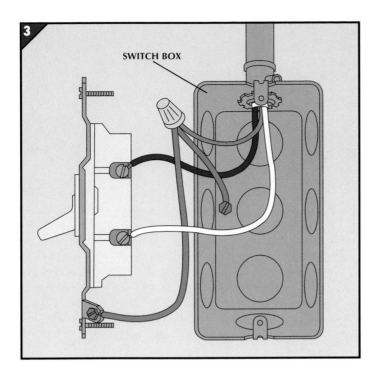

3. Wiring the light switch.

◆ Attach a green jumper wire to the grounding screw in the box and another to the green grounding terminal on the switch strap.

◆ At the switch box, join the bare ground wire of the cable to the two jumper wires.

◆ Connect the black and white cable wires to separate terminals on the switch. Mount the light switch in the switch box and add the cover.

A SWITCH LOOP THAT RUNS THROUGH TWO FIXTURES

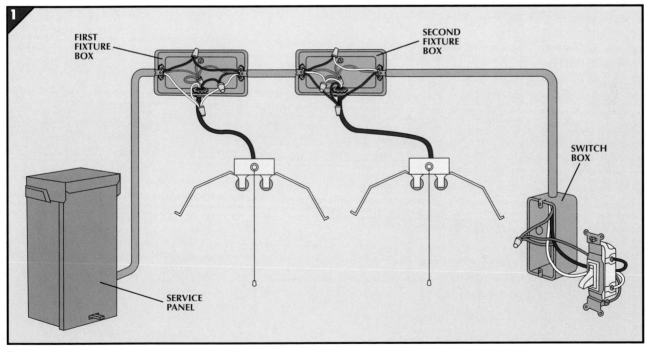

1. Layout of a two-fixture run.

The diagram above shows the wiring for two light fixtures controlled from a single switch. Power from the service panel passes through the first fixture box, on to the second through three-conductor cable, and to the switch. It returns to the second box and then to its fixture. Without three-conductor cable between the fixture boxes the switch could control only the second fixture; the first would be on regardless of the switch position.

◆ Hang the fixtures over the work area, then install a fixture box near each one. Join the fixtures to the boxes with flexible cord (page 62, Step 1).

◆ Install conduit and cable as for a simple one-fixture switch loop (opposite, Step 1), but use three-conductor-with-ground cable between the two fixture boxes.

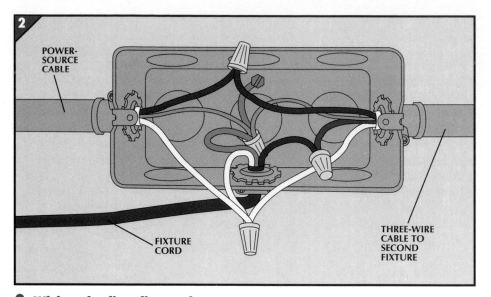

2. Wiring the first fixture box.

◆ At the first fixture box, attach a green jumper wire to the grounding screw.
◆ Connect the bare wires of the two cables to the green jumper wire and the green wire of the fixture cord with a wire cap.
◆ Connect the white wire of the cable from the power source, the white wire going to the second fixture box, and the white wire from the fixture cord.
◆ Join the black wires of the two cables.
◆ Connect the black wire of the fixture cord to the red wire of the cable going to the second fixture box.

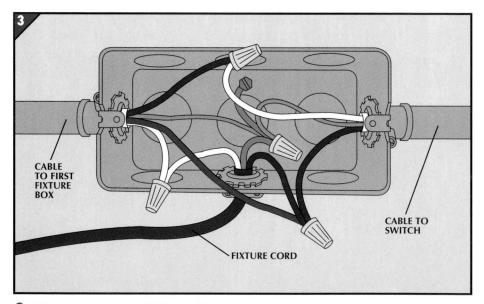

3. Wiring the second fixture box.

◆ Fasten a green jumper wire to the grounding screw in the second fixture box.
◆ With a wire cap connect the bare wires of the two cables to the green jumper, and the green wire of the fixture cord.
◆ Connect the black wire of the cable from the first fixture box to the white wire of the cable going to the switch.
◆ Join the white wire of the cable from the first fixture box to the white wire from the fixture cord.
◆ Connect the red wire of the cable from the first fixture box, the black fixture-cord wire, and the black wire from the cable going to the switch.
◆ Wire the switch *(page 65, Step 3).*

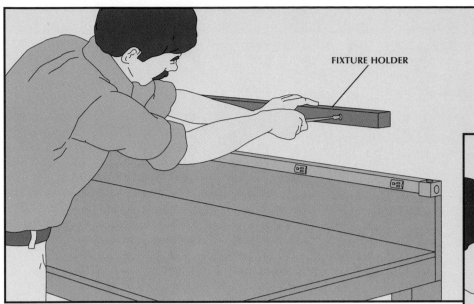

FIXTURE HOLDER

LAMP SHAFT

Mounting a fixture holder.

◆ Draw a level screw-hole line on the wall 9 inches above the table.
◆ For a concrete wall, as shown here, drill holes for screw anchors at 1-foot intervals along the line. Insert the anchors.
◆ Drill corresponding clearance holes along the centerline of a 2-by-2, then secure it with 3-inch No. 8 screws (above).
◆ Fasten the lamp's clamp to the 2-by-2, then fit the lamp in place (inset).

If there is a stud wall behind the bench, nail the strip to each stud with $3\frac{1}{2}$-inch common nails.

TRICKS OF THE TRADE

A Bench Dog for Lamp Support

A workbench with "dog holes" along one edge of the top enables you to fit the holes with metal bench dogs and then clamp a large workpiece between a dog and the vise. You can also use the square dog holes to support a lamp. Bore a hole the same diameter as the lamp shaft into the end of a wood block cut to fit the holes. Position the light at any of the holes along the bench.

If your bench doesn't have dog holes you can bore a hole in a hardwood block and clamp it in the bench vise.

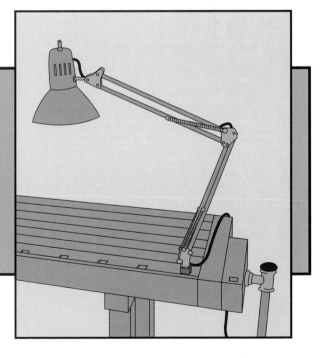

Benches, Jigs, and Accessories

Building your own workbenches, extension tables, and jigs gives you two major advantages over purchasing their commercial counterparts. One, it is much cheaper to construct these items yourself than to buy them ready-made; and two, you can tailor them to suit the kind of work you do, the tools you use, and the layout of your shop.

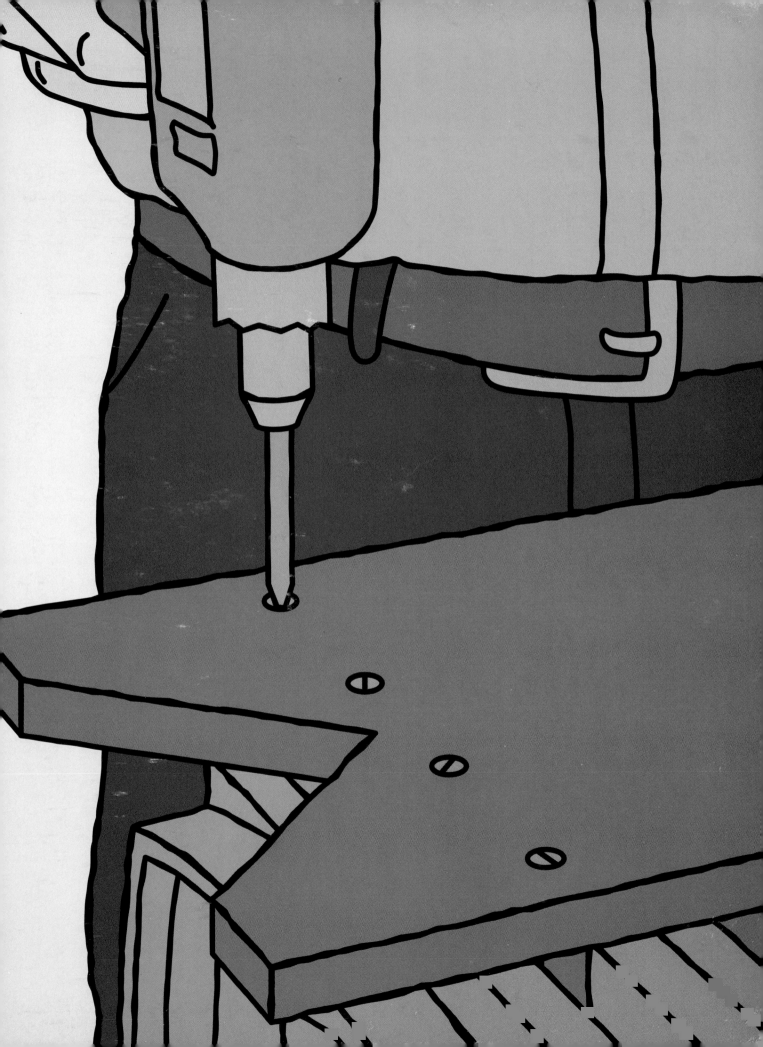

Building a Workbench

The focal point of nearly all shop activity, a workbench is probably the most useful—and most used—tool in any workshop.

Design and Size: Pictured below and described on pages 71 to 81 are five designs. The inexpensive backboard bench is well suited to crafts work. With its broad, unshakable surface and handy tool trough, the woodworking bench is better for heavier, more complex activities. A fold-down table saves space, and a portable bench can be carried to the work. A tall stand not only saves you from having to bend over, but it is also excellent for tasks that require precision.

A full-size bench is between 5 and 7 feet long and between 25 and 35 inches wide, but you can adapt it to the size of the shop and proportions of the owner. Traditionally, a bench is as high as a hip joint, but arm and torso lengths can alter this dimension. The ideal width allows a comfortable reach from front to back, so you can work over the entire top without losing your balance. Leave 3 inches of space beneath the lowest horizontal member so you don't have to lean forward. To fit a bench comfortably in the shop, plan the shop's layout *(pages 44-45)* or position pieces of scrap wood on the floor to simulate the bench.

Special Considerations: For stabilizing a lightweight bench, place weights such as bricks or cement blocks on the lower shelf. You can also fasten the tall stand to the floor with lag bolts and anchors. To protect the working surface, you may want to nail or clamp a sheet of $\frac{1}{2}$-inch medium-density overlay plywood or $\frac{1}{4}$-inch tempered hardboard to the benchtop. A vise is ideal for holding materials in place; for woodworking, line the inner faces of the vise jaws with wood to protect your material.

 TOOLS

Tape measure
Square
Circular saw
Electric drill
  with assorted bits
Hammer
Wood chisel

Mallet
Wrench
Saber saw
Bar clamps
Compass
Sanding block
Rasp
C-clamps

 **MATERIALS**

Lumber (1", 2")
4 x 4 posts
Common nails
  (assorted sizes)
Wood screws
  (assorted sizes)
Lag screws
  and washers
  (assorted sizes)

Carriage bolts and
  washers
  ($\frac{1}{2}$" x $2\frac{1}{2}$", 8")
Wing nuts
Screw anchors
Woodworking vise
Plywood
  ($\frac{1}{4}$", $\frac{1}{2}$", $\frac{3}{4}$")
Wood glue
Sandpaper
  (medium grade)

 **SAFETY TIPS**

Wear goggles when nailing or operating power tools.

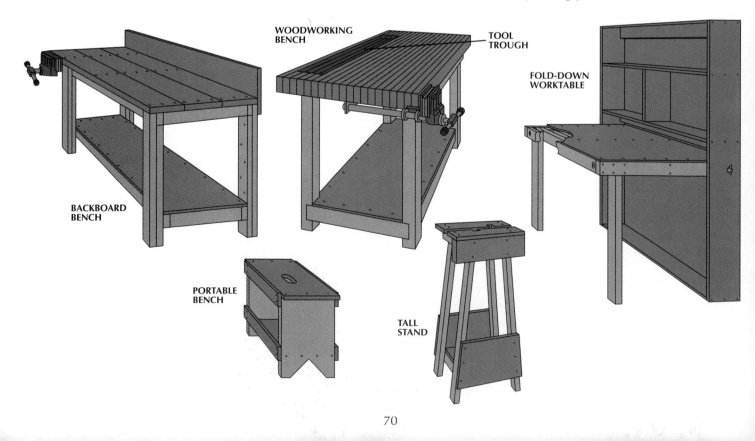

WOODWORKING BENCH

TOOL TROUGH

FOLD-DOWN WORKTABLE

BACKBOARD BENCH

PORTABLE BENCH

TALL STAND

ASSEMBLING A BENCH WITH A BACKBOARD

1. Building the frames.

◆ Prepare each leg by cutting two 2-by-4s—one 5 inches shorter than the planned height of the workbench and the other $1\frac{1}{2}$ inches shorter.

◆ Glue the sections together so the bottom ends are flush, creating a notch at the top.

◆ Drill pilot holes into the shorter pieces, staggering the holes in a zigzag pattern about 4 inches apart.

◆ Drive a $2\frac{1}{2}$-inch No. 8 wood screw into each hole (right).

◆ To support the benchtop, assemble a frame of two 2-by-4s cut 8 inches shorter than the planned length of the top, and three 2-by-4 crosspieces cut 3 inches shorter than its width (inset). Drill pilot holes at the ends and centers of the long boards, then fasten the pieces with glue and 3-inch screws.

◆ Assemble a second frame for the bottom shelf in the same way as the top frame, but make each crosspiece 3 inches shorter than the crosspieces for the top.

NOTCH

CROSSPIECES

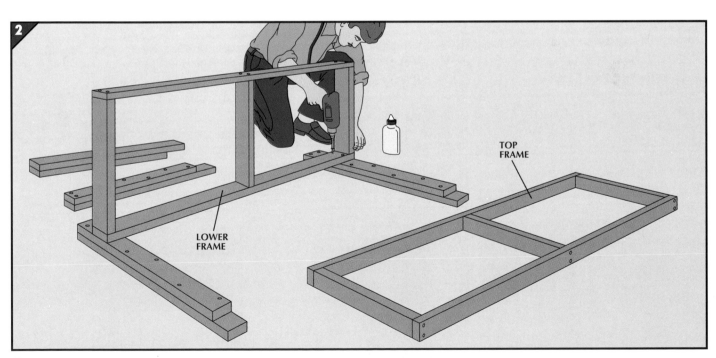

LOWER FRAME

TOP FRAME

2. Assembling the parts.

◆ Lay two of the legs on the floor with their notched faces up, and rest the lower frame against them.

◆ Position the lower frame 3 inches from the bottoms of the legs and flush with their outer edges. Spread glue on the contacting surfaces, then secure the legs to the frame with $2\frac{1}{2}$-inch screws (above).

◆ Turn the assembly over, propping up the free ends of the legs, and join the other side of the frame to the remaining legs in the same way as the first.

◆ Fit the top frame into the notches at the top ends of the legs, making sure it is flush with the ends and outer edges of the legs. Fasten the top frame in place with glue and screws.

OVERHANG

PLYWOOD SHELF

3. Attaching the benchtop.

◆ Cut three 2-by-10s long enough to create a 7-inch overhang for a vise at one end of the top and a 1-inch overhang at the other. Trim one of the boards so the back edge of the top will be flush with the outside of the legs. To save space, you can also make the front edge flush with the legs.

◆ Place the 2-by-10s in position across the top frame. Drill countersunk pilot holes, then fasten the boards to the frame's crosspieces with $2\frac{1}{2}$-inch screws *(left)*.

◆ For the lower shelf, cut a piece of $\frac{1}{2}$-inch plywood to fit over the bottom frame and secure it with glue and $1\frac{1}{2}$-inch common nails.

4. Completing the bench.

◆ With glue and $1\frac{1}{2}$-inch screws, fasten a 2-by-4 to the back of the top frame between the back legs.

◆ With glue and $1\frac{1}{2}$-inch screws, attach a 1-by-12 backboard to the back of the bench, positioning its bottom edge flush with the bottom of the filler 2-by-4 *(right)*.

◆ Position a woodworking vise at the end of the bench with the 7-inch overhang, and mark the locations of the mounting holes. Drill holes at the marks and fasten the vise in place with lag screws appropriate for the size of the vise—typically $\frac{3}{8}$- by $2\frac{1}{2}$-inch screws. If necessary, add blocking so the vise jaw is flush with or slightly below the top *(inset)*.

◆ With medium-grade sandpaper, smooth the top and backboard, and slightly round the sharp corners.

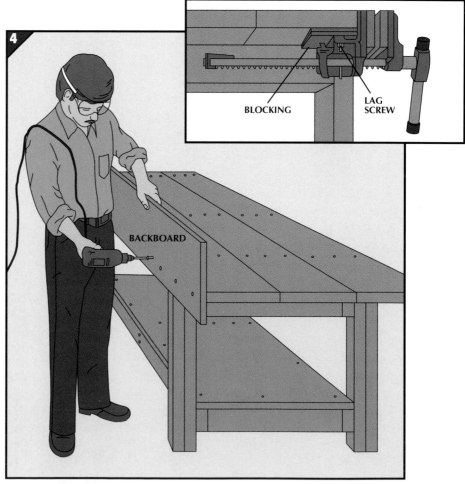

BACKBOARD

BLOCKING

LAG SCREW

CONSTRUCTING A WOODWORKING BENCH

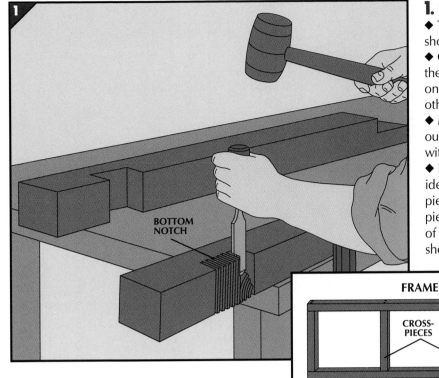

BOTTOM NOTCH

1. Preparing the legs and frames.
◆ To make the legs, cut four 4-by-4s $3\frac{1}{2}$ inches shorter than the desired height of the benchtop.
◆ Outline two notches in each 4-by-4, making them $3\frac{1}{2}$ inches long and $1\frac{1}{2}$ inches deep. Position one notch at the top end of each leg and the other notch 6 inches from the bottom end.
◆ Make a row of $1\frac{1}{2}$-inch-deep cuts across each outline with a circular saw. Remove the waste with a mallet and chisel (left).
◆ From 2-by-4 lumber, cut pieces to form two identical frames with four evenly spaced crosspieces (inset). Make the front and back frame pieces 1 foot shorter than the planned length of the benchtop; cut the crosspieces 7 inches shorter than the planned width of the top.

◆ Drill pilot holes, then assemble the frames with glue and $2\frac{1}{2}$-inch No. 8 wood screws.

FRAME

CROSS-PIECES

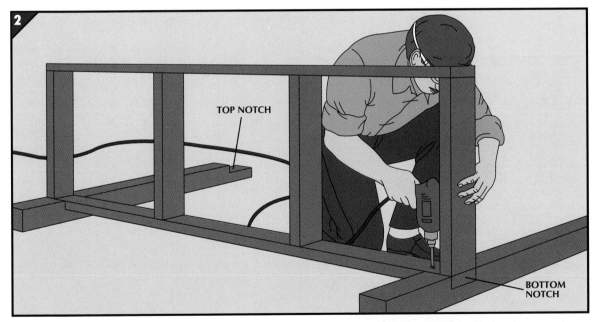

TOP NOTCH

BOTTOM NOTCH

2. Attaching the legs.
◆ Lay two legs on the floor and set one frame into the lower notches, aligning the ends of the frame with the outsides of the legs.
◆ Drill two $\frac{3}{8}$-inch pilot holes through the frame and about $\frac{1}{2}$ inch into the leg at notches, then drill $\frac{1}{2}$-inch clearance holes through the frame (above).
◆ With a wrench, tighten a $\frac{1}{2}$- by 3-inch lag screw, with a washer, into each hole, securing the frame to the legs.

◆ Turn the frame over and attach the two remaining legs to the other side.
◆ Secure the top frame in the upper notches with lag screws, making sure it is flush with the outer faces of the top.
◆ Cut a piece of $\frac{1}{2}$-inch plywood for the lower shelf, notching it at the corners to fit around the legs. Nail the shelf in place with 2-inch common nails.

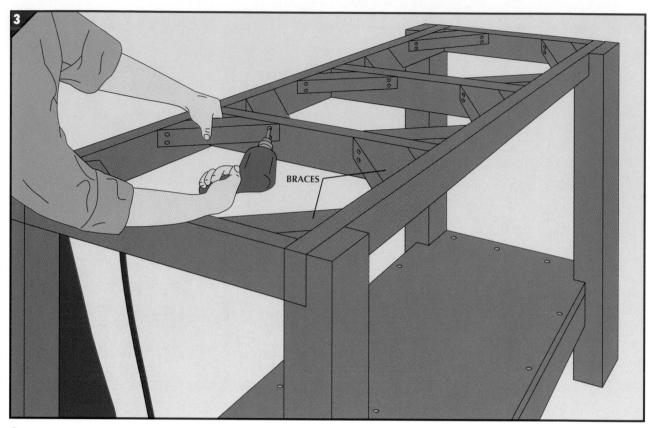

3. Adding braces.

◆ Cut 12 2-by-4 braces to fit into the corners of the top frame, mitering their ends at 45 degrees so their long edges are about $11\frac{1}{2}$ inches long.

◆ Hold the braces with their tops flush with the top of the frame and drill pilot holes for 3-inch screws.

◆ Fasten the braces to the frame with glue and screws *(above)*.

4. Cutting the top pieces.

◆ The top is made from 2-by-4s glued together face to face and set on edge. To calculate the number of 2-by-4s needed, divide the planned width of the bench by $1\frac{1}{2}$ and round the result up to the nearest whole number.

◆ Square one end of each 2-by-4, and trim one of them to the planned length of the benchtop.

◆ Nail a piece of scrap wood to one end of the trimmed 2-by-4 as a stop block *(right)*, and use the assembly to mark the remaining 2-by-4s for cutting.

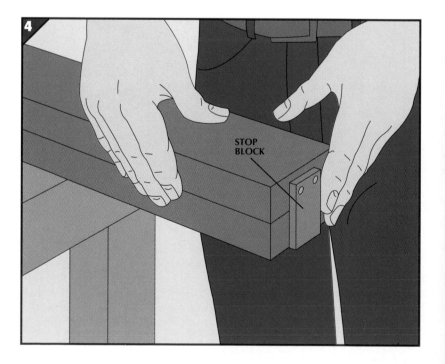

5. Notching the benchtop.

◆ To fashion a storage trough for tools in the benchtop, draw a line on the face of one 2-by-4, 2 inches from the top edge. Next, make marks on the top edge 8 inches from each end and connect them to the first line at 45-degree angles.

◆ Cut along the line with a saber saw, creating a long notch.

◆ Use this board as a template to mark and cut identical notches in three additional top pieces *(right)*.

◆ To notch the front edge of the benchtop to hold a vise, align two pieces and clamp them together, then measure the size of the vise mount and transfer its measurements to one end of the clamped 2-by-4s. Notch the 2-by-4s along the marked lines. Be sure the notch is cut deeply enough so that the vise will be flush with or slightly below the surface of the bench. Test-fit the vise and mark its bolt-hole locations on the clamped boards *(inset)*.

NOTCH
BOLT HOLES
VISE MOUNT

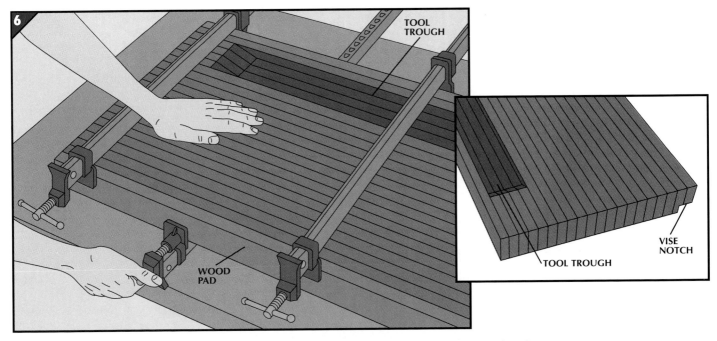

TOOL TROUGH

WOOD PAD

TOOL TROUGH
VISE NOTCH

6. Gluing up the top.

◆ Extend three bar clamps and lay them face up on a work surface.

◆ Starting with the two boards notched for the vise, spread a wavy bead of glue on the face of the first piece, butt the second board against it with the ends aligned, and lay them on the bar clamps. Position the clamps at each end and in the middle of the boards.

◆ Repeat with the remaining boards, ending with the four notched for the trough, so the top is configured as shown in the inset. Place long wood pads on each side, then snug up the clamps.

◆ Turn the assembly over and add two clamps, centered between the others *(above)*.

For a wide bench, assemble the top as two halves, then glue the two slabs together.

7. Bolting the top to the bracing.

◆ Drill two $\frac{1}{2}$-inch clearance holes through each brace.

◆ Set the top on the frame so it overhangs the frame equally front and back, 11 inches at the vise end, and about 1 inch at the other end.

◆ Drill a $\frac{3}{8}$-inch pilot hole through each clearance hole in each brace—except those under the tool trough—2 inches up into the top. Beneath the trough, drill to a depth of only 1 inch.

◆ With a wrench, drive a $\frac{1}{2}$- by $2\frac{1}{2}$-inch lag screw with a washer into each hole under the tool trough. Drive $3\frac{1}{2}$-inch lag screws into the other holes.

◆ Once all the screws are in place, tighten them further to pull the top down securely against the frame (right).

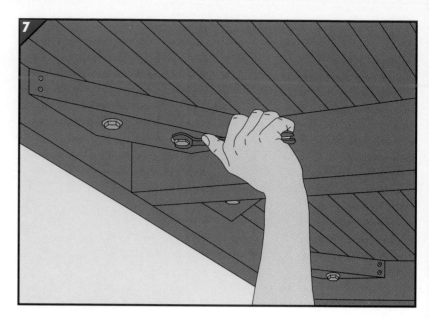

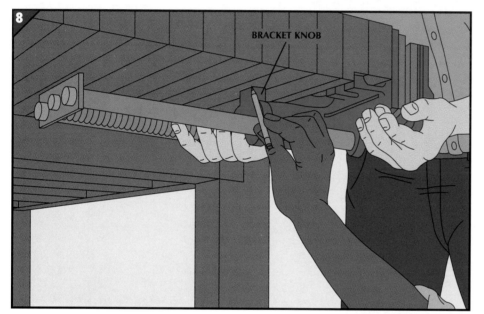

BRACKET KNOB

8. Installing the vise.

◆ If the vise has a projecting bracket knob, have a helper hold the vise in place while you mark the knob's position (left); then cut out a recess for the knob by drilling $\frac{1}{2}$-inch holes within its outline, and cutting out the waste with a chisel.

◆ Mark the bolt-hole positions, then drill a $\frac{3}{8}$-inch pilot hole into the top at each mark.

◆ Secure the vise with $\frac{3}{8}$- by 2-inch lag screws.

TRICKS OF THE TRADE

A Quick-Switch Vise

Many woodworking vises are not suitable for gripping metal. But rather than bolting a metal vise to your bench, attach it instead to a T-shaped base made from two pieces of $\frac{3}{4}$-inch plywood joined together with a dado joint and screws. The assembly can be clamped in the woodworking vise whenever it is needed (right).

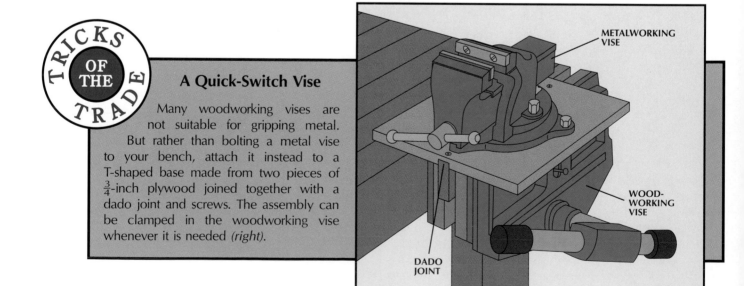

METALWORKING VISE

WOOD-WORKING VISE

DADO JOINT

FASHIONING A FOLD-DOWN WORKTABLE

1. Constructing the wall frame.

◆ Cut four 1-by-8s to form a 6-foot-high box with an interior width of $46\frac{1}{2}$ inches. Butt the sides against the top and bottom, and fasten the assembly together with glue and $1\frac{1}{2}$-inch No. 6 wood screws. Secure two 1-by-8 shelves to the upper half of the frame, with the lower shelf about 6 inches above the planned height of the work surface. Center a 1-by-8 vertically between the shelves. Cut a back panel for the frame from $\frac{1}{4}$-inch plywood and secure it to the frame's back edges with $1\frac{1}{2}$-inch common nails.

◆ On the wall, mark the studs at the planned bench location, then place the frame against the wall so the sides align with studs, and transfer the stud marks to the front of the back panel. Position a 2-by-4 horizontally under the lower shelf, then drill two pilot holes through the board at each stud mark and drive $\frac{1}{4}$- by 4-inch lag screws to anchor the frame to the studs. In a masonry wall, drive screws into screw anchors. Repeat with a 2-by-4 set under the top of the frame.

◆ Drill $\frac{1}{2}$-inch pivot holes through the frame sides, 1 inch out from the wall and 2 inches below the planned height of the work surface.

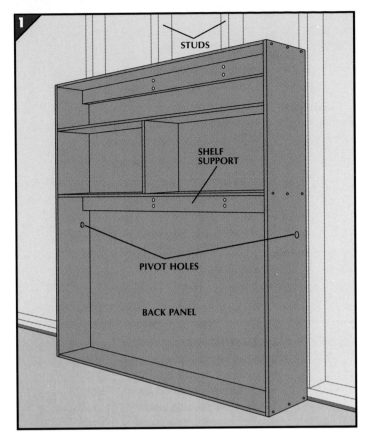

2. Shaping the bench supports.

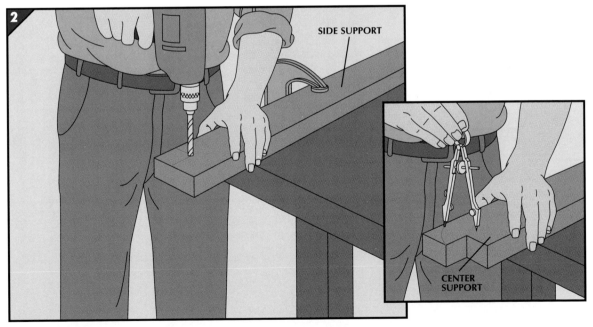

◆ For the side supports, cut two 2-by-4s long enough to span from the bottom of the frame to a point 1 inch above the pivot hole. Mark a $1\frac{1}{2}$-inch square at one corner of each 2-by-4, then drill a $\frac{1}{2}$-inch hole through the inside corner of each square *(above)*.

◆ For the center support, cut a third 2-by-4, $7\frac{5}{8}$ inches shorter than the others, and cut out a $1\frac{1}{2}$-inch notch at one end. Adjust a compass to a 2-inch radius, set the point 2 inches from the notched end, centered between the edges of the board, and scribe an arc at the corner *(inset)*.

◆ Mark the same arc on the side supports at the marked corners, then cut the arcs on all three pieces with a saber saw and sand them smooth.

3. Adding the crosspieces.

◆ Subtract $3\frac{1}{4}$ inches from the inside width of the wall frame. Cut one 2-by-2 and three 2-by-4 crosspieces to this length; set two of the 2-by-4s aside.

◆ Place the side supports on the floor on edge, rounded corners down. Locate the notched center support between the other two.

◆ Seat the 2-by-2 crosspiece in the notch of the center support with its ends flush against the side supports. Fasten it to the supports with glue and 3-inch No. 6 screws, then glue and screw a 2-by-4 crosspiece between the two side supports (*right*) and against the bottom end of the center support.

◆ Fasten a 2-by-4 brace horizontally between the center support and each side support, centered between the two crosspieces.

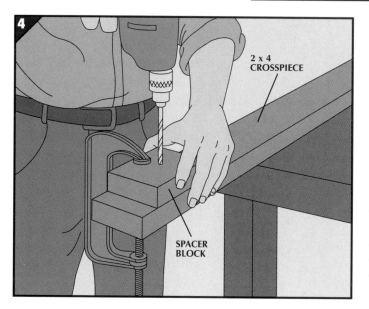

2 x 2 CROSSPIECE

NOTCH

CENTER SUPPORT

BRACE

2 x 4 CROSSPIECE

SIDE SUPPORT

4. Preparing the folding leg assembly.

◆ From 2-by-4 stock, cut two spacer blocks $3\frac{1}{2}$ inches long, and drill a $\frac{1}{2}$-inch hole through the center of each one. Clamp a spacer block at each end of one of the remaining 2-by-4 crosspieces, 1 inch from the ends, and drill through the board, guided by the spacer blocks (*left*). Repeat with the final crosspiece.

◆ Cut two legs from 2-by-4 stock, $\frac{1}{2}$ inch shorter than the planned height of the work surface. With the spacer block flush with the end, drill a $\frac{1}{2}$-inch hole through one end of each leg.

◆ Using the technique on page 77, Step 2, round the inside top corner of each leg so it will clear the top when it is folded up.

2 x 4 CROSSPIECE

SPACER BLOCK

5. Assembling the legs.

◆ Glue and screw a spacer block to one end of each crosspiece, aligning the holes. Stack the crosspieces and the legs as shown at right, inserting a $\frac{1}{2}$- by 8-inch carriage bolt through the holes and adding washers on each side of the legs.

◆ Temporarily tighten a nut over the assembly.

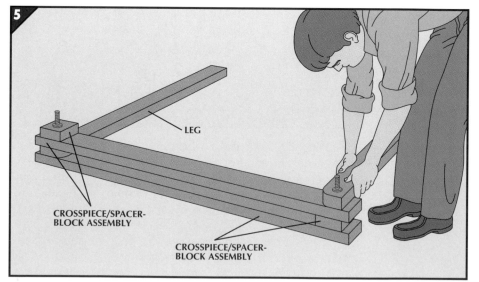

LEG

CROSSPIECE/SPACER-BLOCK ASSEMBLY

CROSSPIECE/SPACER-BLOCK ASSEMBLY

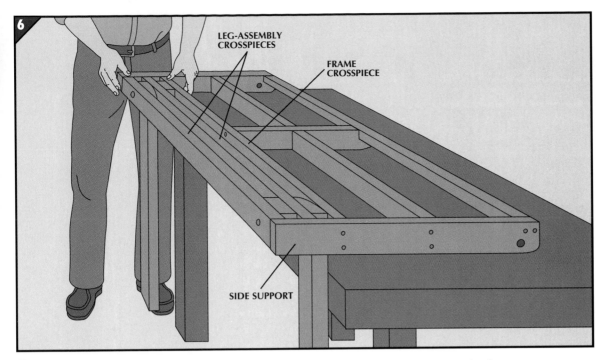

LEG-ASSEMBLY CROSSPIECES

FRAME CROSSPIECE

SIDE SUPPORT

6. Attaching the legs to the frame.

◆ Position the leg assembly in front of the frame crosspiece, holding the top edges of both assemblies flush.

◆ Mark the points where the leg-assembly bolts touch the frame crosspiece. Drill a $\frac{1}{2}$-inch hole at each mark, remove the nuts, and slide the bolts through the holes *(above)*.

Hand-tighten the bolts to snug the leg assembly against the frame crosspiece.

◆ Drill pilot holes and screw the leg-assembly crosspieces to the side supports of the bench frame.

◆ Tighten the bolts so the legs will swing down with only slight resistance.

7. Installing the bench frame.

◆ Swing the legs down and align the pivot holes in the sides of the bench frame with their holes in the wall frame.

◆ Place washers between the two frames, and thread $\frac{1}{2}$- by $2\frac{1}{2}$-inch carriage bolts through the holes with the boltheads on the inside.

◆ Tighten each bolt with a washer and wing nut.

◆ Tighten the wing nuts firmly when the bench is in use, and loosen them slightly to pivot the entire bench assembly, with legs folded, back into the wall frame.

Complete the benchtop by covering the work surface with a piece of $\frac{1}{2}$-inch plywood, secured with glue and countersunk $1\frac{1}{4}$-inch No. 6 wood screws.

MAKING A PORTABLE WORKBENCH

1. Assembling the bench.

◆ Cut two 18-inch-high legs from 1-by-12 lumber and saw a triangular notch 4 inches high and 8 inches wide from the bottom of each piece.

◆ Cut a 25-inch-long 1-by-12 shelf and clamp it end-up in a vise, flush with the top of the workbench.

◆ Position a leg against the shelf so the bottom of the shelf aligns with the top of the leg cutout. Drill three pilot holes through the leg into the shelf, secure the shelf with glue and 2-inch No. 6 wood screws, and attach the other leg in the same way *(right)*.

◆ Center a 30-inch-long 1-by-12 astride the legs as a top, then glue and screw it in place.

◆ Fasten two pairs of 1-by-3 aprons to the sides of the legs *(inset)* so the upper edges of one pair are flush with the top and the lower edges of the other pair are flush with the bottom of the shelf.

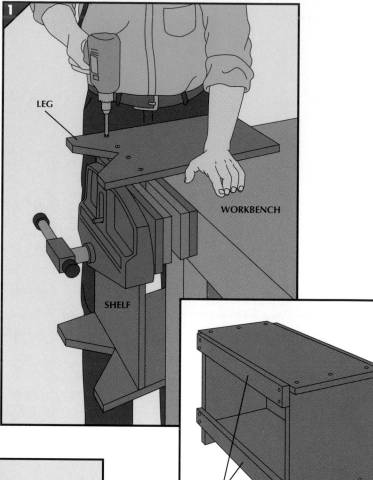

2. Completing the bench.

◆ Outline an oval handgrip on the top 4 inches long and $1\frac{1}{2}$ inches wide.

◆ Drill a $\frac{3}{8}$-inch hole within the oval for the blade of a saber saw or a keyhole saw and cut out the oval *(left)*.

◆ Work off any rough spots with a rasp, then smooth the opening with medium-grade sandpaper.

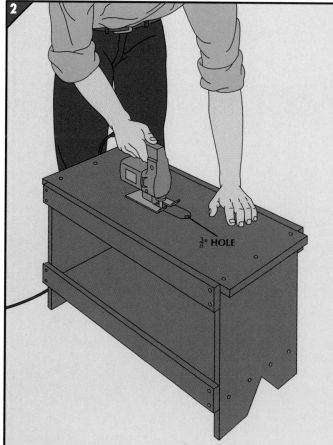

A TALL STAND FOR SMALL JOBS

1. Making the leg frames.
◆ From 2-by-4s, cut four waist-high legs and four 17-inch-long cross braces.
◆ With wood glue and $2\frac{1}{2}$-inch No. 8 wood screws, fasten a brace across the top of one pair of legs, aligning the ends of the braces with the tops and outside edges of the legs.
◆ Flip the assembly over and fasten a second brace $4\frac{1}{2}$ inches above the bottom of the legs. Fasten braces to the second pair of legs in the same manner (right).

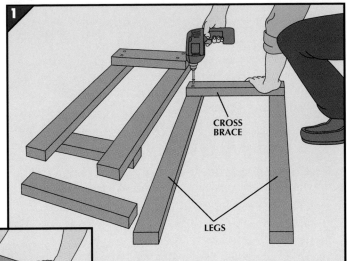

CROSS BRACE

LEGS

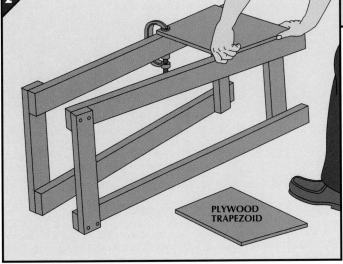

PLYWOOD TRAPEZOID

2. Assembling the leg frames.
◆ Cut two trapezoidal panels from $\frac{3}{4}$-inch plywood so they measure 12 inches high, 15 inches along the top, and 17 inches along the bottom.
◆ To fasten a panel to the leg frames, first apply glue, then clamp the panel in place, flush with the outside edges of the legs (left). Screw the assembly together, then flip it over and attach a panel to the other side of the legs.

3. Completing the bench.
◆ For the benchtop, cut two pieces of 1-inch-thick hardwood to a width of 8 inches. Cut the pieces long enough to straddle the leg assembly flush with the outside of the cross braces; make them longer for an overhang.
◆ Clamp the pieces together in a vise and cut a 1-inch-square notch out of the edges, 6 inches from one end, with a saw and a chisel (page 73, Step 1).
◆ Lay the top pieces across the leg assembly and at right angles to the cross braces, positioning their notches at opposite ends and leaving a 1-inch gap between them, which will later allow you to fit clamps into the top (inset).
◆ Drill countersunk pilot holes through the top boards and anchor

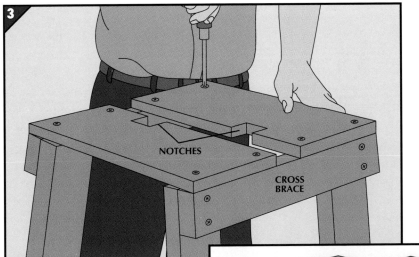

NOTCHES

CROSS BRACE

them with $2\frac{1}{2}$-inch screws (above).
◆ Fasten a $\frac{1}{2}$-inch plywood shelf across the lower cross braces with glue and $1\frac{1}{2}$-inch common nails.

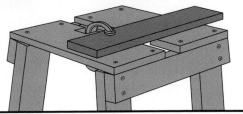

Adding Accessories to Power Tools

Shop-made accessories can increase the efficiency and versatility of many workshop tools. Although commercial tables and jigs are available, you can save money and tailor the accessories to your needs by building them yourself.

Work-Surface Extensions: To support panels and long boards at a stationary saw, use extension tables or roller stands. For general-purpose cutting with a table saw, place extensions on one side of the blade *(below and pages 83-85)*. For ripping 4- by 8-foot panels, however, you may prefer to extend the table by 2 feet on both sides of the blade; to crosscut very long boards, set up an even wider extension. For ripping on a table saw, band saw, or radial-arm saw, you'll need a roller stand at the outfeed side of the saw *(page 86)*.

Because a radial-arm saw is often placed against a wall, its extension table can be as long as the available space—doubling as a work counter. It can be screwed to the wall and supported by legs along the outside edge.

Jigs: Shop-built "third hands" for specific tasks can make your work safer and more accurate. For a table saw, you can fashion crosscut, miter, and tenoning jigs *(pages 87-89)*, as well as featherboards and push sticks *(page 90)*. A shop-built drill-press table simplifies angled work *(page 91)*.

 TOOLS

Tape measure
Carpenter's level
Carpenter's square
Circular saw
Saber saw
C-clamps

Electric drill
Spade bit (1")
Counterbore bit
Hacksaw
Wrench
Screwdriver
Combination square
Hand-screw clamp

 **MATERIALS**

Lumber (1", 2", 4")
Plywood ($\frac{3}{4}$")
Common nails ($1\frac{1}{4}$")
Wood screws ($\frac{7}{8}$" No. 6; $1\frac{1}{4}$", $1\frac{1}{2}$", $1\frac{3}{4}$", 2", $2\frac{1}{4}$", $2\frac{1}{2}$" No. 8)
Threaded rods ($\frac{1}{4}$"), washers, lock washers and nuts

Carriage bolts ($\frac{1}{4}$" x $2\frac{1}{2}$"), washers, wing nuts
Hanger bolts ($\frac{7}{16}$" x 2"), washers, wing nuts
Wood glue
Roller assembly
Clear polycarbonate sheet
Casters
Toggle clamp
Butt hinges (3")

SAFETY TIPS

Wear goggles when nailing or operating a power tool.

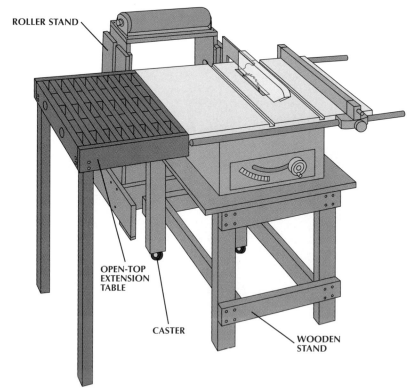

ROLLER STAND
OPEN-TOP EXTENSION TABLE
CASTER
WOODEN STAND

Table-saw extensions.

Shop-built accessories hold a table saw at a convenient height and extend its working surface *(left)*; they can be adapted for use with other power tools as well. To support the saw, build a wooden stand 32 to 42 inches high, basing its design on the wheeled table on page 47, or on one of the workbenches on pages 70 to 79. To enable a nonwheeled type to be moved easily, you can shorten two of its legs and add casters. An open-top extension table bolted to the saw table will steady a sheet of plywood or a long board during crosscutting. A freestanding roller stand—positioned on the outfeed side of the saw at a right angle to the direction in which you push the work—will support long boards during rip cutting.

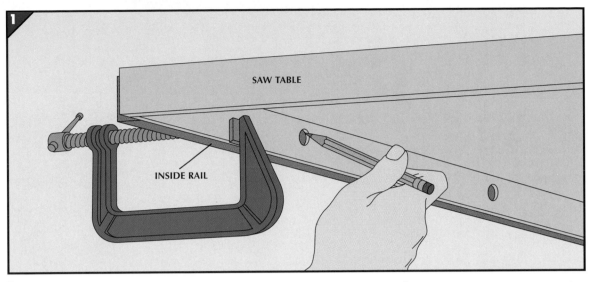

1. Establishing hole locations.

◆ To make an extension table for a table saw, start with the inside rail that will abut the edge of the saw table, and cut a 1-by-2 rail $1\frac{1}{2}$ inches shorter than the edge.

◆ Clamp the rail to the edge of the saw table with its top flush with the top of the table. On the rail, mark the holes along the table's edge *(above)*.

◆ Counterbore a $\frac{3}{8}$-inch-deep hole at each mark with a 1-inch spade bit, then drill through the center of the holes with a $\frac{5}{16}$-inch twist bit.

◆ For every $1\frac{1}{2}$ inches of extension table width you want to add, cut one rail to the same length as the inside rail and two 4-inch 1-by-2 spacer blocks.

◆ Cut a 1-by-4 outside rail the same length as the other rails.

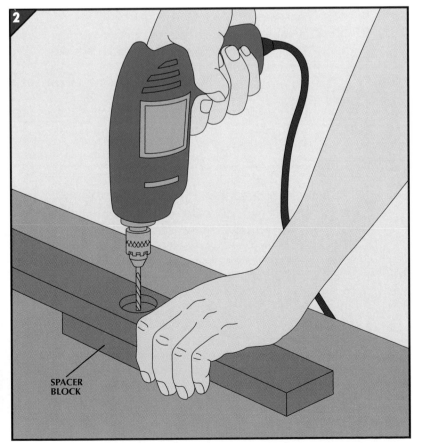

2. Preparing the rails.

◆ Center a spacer block under one of the holes in the inside rail and line up the edges of the two pieces. Drill a matching hole through the spacer block *(left)*.

◆ Use the spacer block as a guide to bore holes in the remaining blocks; use the inside rail as a guide for drilling $\frac{5}{16}$-inch holes through the other rails. Mark the top of each piece after drilling it so the holes can be lined up quickly when you assemble the table.

◆ Counterbore the outside rail as you did the inside rail.

◆ With a hacksaw, cut two $\frac{1}{4}$-inch threaded rods 1 inch longer than the extension-table width; put a washer and a nut on one end of each rod.

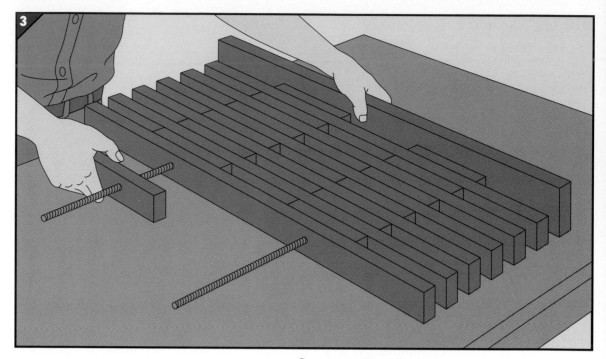

3. Assembling the top.

◆ Set the top edge of the outside rail on a flat surface and slide the rods through its holes.

◆ Thread the rest of the spacers and rails onto the rods, spreading a thin coat of wood glue on both sides of the spacer blocks as you go.

◆ Slip on the inside rail so its counterbored surface will butt against the saw table.

◆ Put a washer and a nut onto the outer ends of both rods, seating them in the counterbored cavities.

◆ With the assembly perfectly flat, tighten the nuts until the glue begins to squeeze out and about 1 inch of threaded rod extends from the holes in the inside rail.

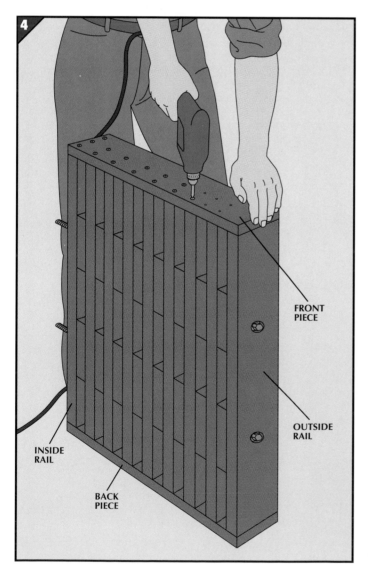

INSIDE
RAIL

BACK
PIECE

FRONT
PIECE

OUTSIDE
RAIL

4. Attaching the table ends.

◆ For the front and back of the extension table, cut two 1-by-4s as long as its width.

◆ Holding one piece so its top edge is flush with the extension-table top, drill pilot holes through the board into the end of each rail.

◆ Spread glue on the rail ends and secure the piece with $1\frac{1}{2}$-inch No. 8 wood screws.

◆ Attach the piece on the other side in the same manner (left).

◆ Slide the protruding ends of the threaded rods through the holes in the side of the saw table and prop up the other end of the extension table so it is level.

◆ Cut two 2-by-2 legs $1\frac{1}{2}$ inches shorter than the height of the extension-tabletop.

5. Attaching the legs.

◆ Holding a leg inside one corner of the extension table, drill four staggered pilot holes through the frame pieces and into the leg.

◆ Attach the leg with 2-inch screws *(right)*. Fasten the other leg in the same way.

◆ Under the saw table, thread a lock washer and a nut onto each of the threaded rods and firmly tighten the nuts.

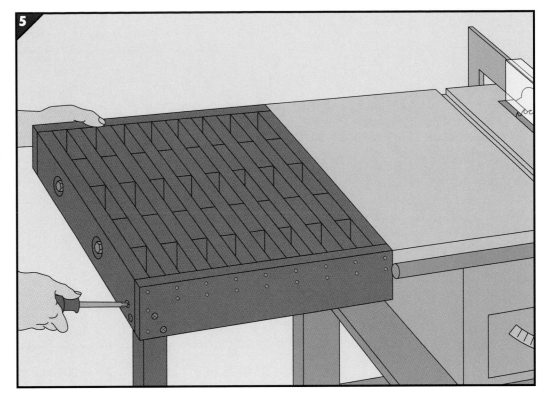

EXTENDING A RADIAL-ARM SAW

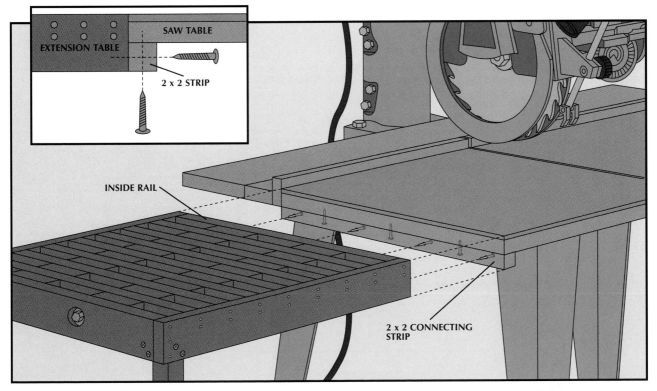

EXTENSION TABLE

SAW TABLE

2 x 2 STRIP

INSIDE RAIL

2 x 2 CONNECTING STRIP

Anchoring the table.

Since the typical radial-arm saw lacks a convenient edge for bolting on an extension table, attach a permanent 2-by-2 connecting strip to the saw table.

◆ Build the extension table to the desired height and width as for a table saw *(pages 83-85, Steps 1-5)*.

◆ Cut a 2-by-2 to the same length as the extension table's inside rail, drill pilot holes for $2\frac{1}{2}$-inch No. 8 wood screws through the 2-by-2 and into the underside of the saw table, and fasten it in place.

◆ To attach the extension table, position it against the saw table and drill pilot holes for $2\frac{1}{4}$-inch screws through the 2-by-2 and into the inside rail, then screw the pieces together *(inset)*.

MAKING A ROLLER STAND

1. Building the base.

◆ Cut two 30-inch-long uprights from 1-by-6 stock. Starting at one end, cut a 14-inch-long, $\frac{1}{4}$-inch-wide slot down the middle of each upright with a saber saw.

◆ Cut two rails $19\frac{1}{2}$ inches long and a crosspiece and two feet 18 inches long.

◆ Tack $\frac{3}{4}$- by $\frac{3}{4}$- by 3-inch pads to the underside of the feet to keep the stand from wobbling.

◆ Aligning the pieces with a carpenter's square, hold a foot and an upright in a perfect "T." Drill pilot holes through the joint, and fasten the pieces together with $1\frac{1}{4}$-inch No. 8 wood screws. Join the opposite foot and upright in the same way.

◆ Fasten the rails to the uprights, making sure that they are perpendicular to each other.

◆ Attach the crosspiece to the uprights just below the slots (right).

◆ As a guide for the roller frame, cut $\frac{3}{4}$- by $\frac{3}{4}$-inch cleats as tracks. With glue and $1\frac{1}{4}$-inch common nails, fix the cleats to the uprights about $\frac{1}{4}$ inch from the outside edges.

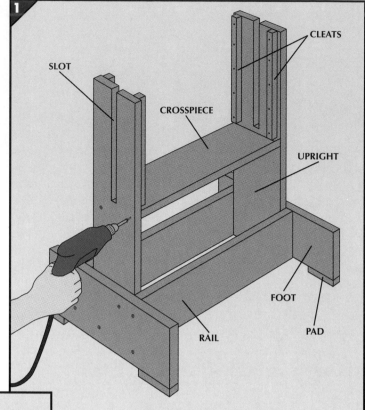

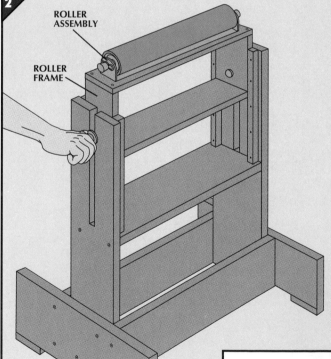

2. Adding the roller frame.

◆ From 1-by-4 stock, cut four pieces to construct a 10- by 18-inch frame for the roller. Assemble the frame with glue and $1\frac{1}{4}$-inch screws.

◆ Screw the roller assembly to the frame or, instead of a roller assembly, fasten plate-mounted casters or commercial roller balls (inset) to the frame.

◆ Bore a $\frac{1}{4}$-inch hole in the middle of each side of the frame and about 3 inches from the bottom, and push $\frac{1}{4}$- by $2\frac{1}{2}$-inch carriage bolts through the holes from the inside out.

◆ Lower the frame into the tracks so the carriage bolts slide down the slots. Set the roller at the desired height, then add a washer and a wing nut to each carriage bolt; tighten the nuts to hold the roller in position (left).

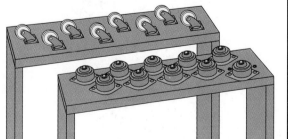

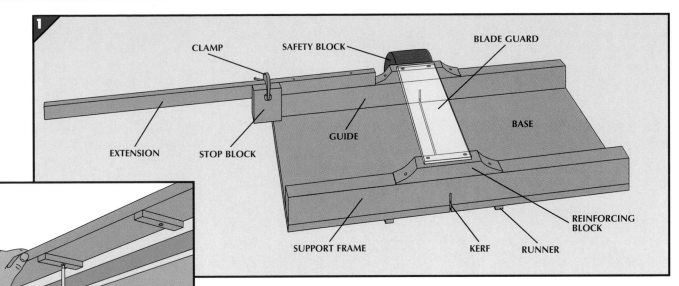

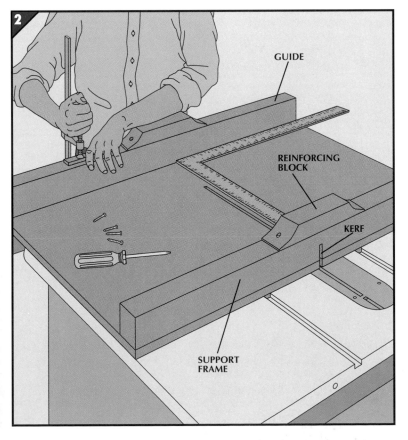

1. Attaching the runners.

A jig like the one above will help you make accurate crosscuts with a table saw.

◆ From $\frac{3}{4}$-inch plywood, cut the base 25 inches deep and as wide as the saw table, but no wider than 36 inches.
◆ Cut two 25-inch-long hardwood runners to fit the saw table's miter slots.

◆ Drill countersunk pilot holes 3 inches from each end of the runners.
◆ Place the runners in the miter slots and slide them out to overhang the back end of the table. Position the base squarely over the runners and fasten it with $\frac{7}{8}$-inch No. 6 wood screws (inset). Slide the base forward and drive in the screws at the front end.

2. Completing the jig.

◆ Cut the support frame and guide from 2-by-4 stock to the width of the base.
◆ From a 2-by-2, cut the reinforcing blocks 8 inches long; with glue and $1\frac{1}{4}$-inch screws, fasten the blocks to the middle of the guide and support frame.
◆ Align the support frame along the back edge of the base, drill countersunk pilot holes through the base into the support, and fasten the pieces together with $1\frac{3}{4}$-inch No. 8 screws.
◆ With the runners in the miter slots, turn on the saw and cut a kerf through the support frame and three-quarters of the way across the base. Turn off the saw and lower the blade below the table.
◆ Using a carpenter's square, align the guide along the front edge of the base square to the saw kerf, then clamp it in place (left). Screw the guide to the base from underneath.
◆ From a 4-by-4, cut the safety block 6 inches long, round off the top edge, and paint it red. Glue it to the guide, centered on the kerf.
◆ Raise the saw blade and finish the kerf across the base, cutting just far enough into the safety block so the top of the blade contacts the guide.
◆ Screw a clear polycarbonate blade guard to the reinforcing blocks.

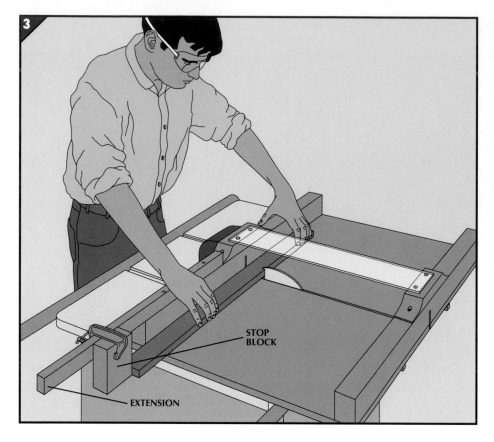

3. Crosscutting with the jig.

◆ To hold the workpiece in position while making several crosscuts to the same length, screw a 1-by-2 extension to the right side of the guide and clamp a stop block to the extension.

◆ With the workpiece against the guide and the cutting mark aligned with the blade, adjust the stop block to rest against the end of the board and clamp it in place.

◆ Make the cut by holding the workpiece firmly against the guide and the stop block and sliding the jig forward, feeding the workpiece into the blade *(left)*.

STOP BLOCK

EXTENSION

GUIDING MITER CUTS

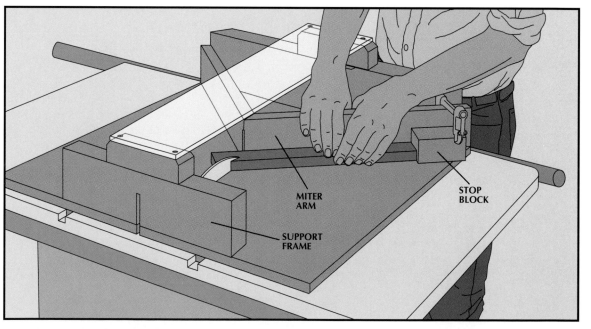

MITER ARM

STOP BLOCK

SUPPORT FRAME

Building and using the jig.

◆ Construct a crosscut jig *(page 87, Steps 1 and 2)*, but make the base 24 by 24 inches, and cut the support frame and guide from 2-by-6 stock. Make the frame short enough so as not to interfere with long workpieces.

◆ Cut 17-inch-long miter arms from 1-by-4s, beveling one end of each arm at 45 degrees. Butt the beveled ends together, centered over

the kerf. Check with a combination square that each arm is at 45 degrees to the kerf, then screw them to the base from underneath.

◆ With the workpiece against the miter arm and the cutting mark lined up with the blade, butt a stop block against the piece and clamp it to the arm. Push the jig toward the blade *(above)*. Make mating miter cuts on the other arm.

Held against the rip fence of a table saw, an adjustable tapering jig allows you to repeat identical tapered cuts along the lengths of boards. The two legs of the jig are connected by a hinge, and a sliding adjustment bracket locks to set the legs at the desired taper. Reference lines on the taper scale allow you to measure the amount of taper in terms of inches per foot. A stop to hold the workpiece is fixed to one leg at the unhinged end. The workpiece is butted against the stop, then the jig is pushed with the handle past the saw blade.

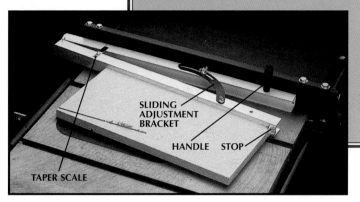

SLIDING ADJUSTMENT BRACKET

HANDLE   STOP

TAPER SCALE

A TENONING JIG

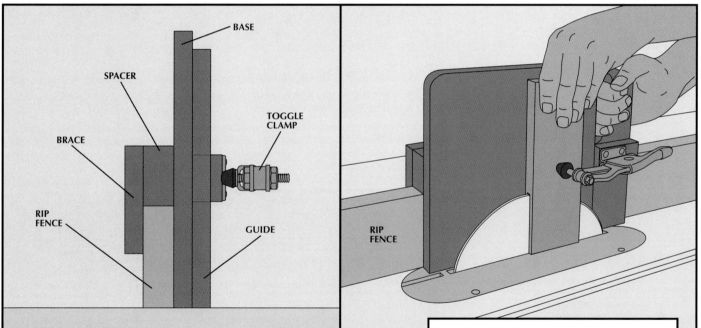

BASE

SPACER

BRACE

TOGGLE CLAMP

RIP FENCE

GUIDE

RIP FENCE

Building the jig.

◆ From $\frac{3}{4}$-inch plywood, cut a 9- by 12-inch base and a 4- by 12-inch brace (above, left).

◆ With a saber saw, cut a hand-hold in one corner of the base, as shown above, right.

◆ Cut an 8-inch-long 1-by-2 guide board and screw it vertically to the base in front of the opening.

◆ Fasten a toggle clamp to a block slightly thicker than the guide, then screw the block to the base against the guide.

◆ Cut a spacer as thick as the rip fence, 2 inches wide and 12 inches long.

◆ Screw the spacer to the base so that the spacer rests on the fence when the base rests on the saw table. Then fasten the brace to the spacer.

To cut a mortise or a tenon, place the jig astride the rip fence and clamp the workpiece to the base against the guide. Adjust the rip fence to align the cutting mark with the blade, then slide the jig along the fence. A commercial jig (photograph) works in a similar way.

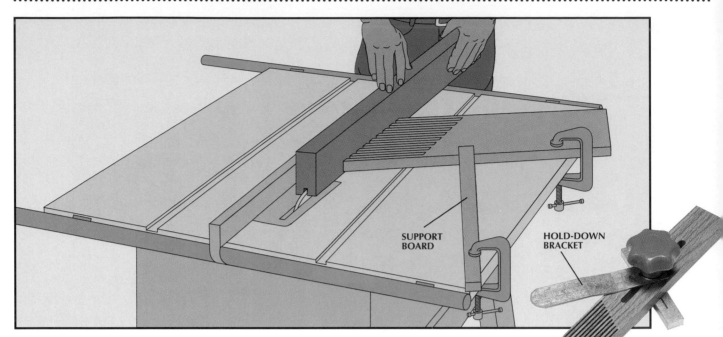

A featherboard.

With its springy fingers, a featherboard presses a workpiece against the rip fence while letting it slide smoothly past the blade *(above)*, reducing risk of kickback. The commercial model *(photograph)* fits in the miter slot; turning the knob tightens it in place and lowers the hold-down bracket against the workpiece.

◆ From a $\frac{3}{4}$-inch piece of straight-grained hardwood, cut a piece about 6 inches wide and 16 inches long.

◆ Miter one end at a 45- to 60-degree angle, then cut

a series of 5-inch-long kerfs from the mitered end at $\frac{1}{8}$-inch intervals, creating the fingers. Cut a $\frac{1}{2}$- by 1-inch notch along the middle of the long edge.

To use the featherboard, place the workpiece against the fence and clamp the featherboard against it on the infeed side of the blade. Clamp a support board in the notch. *(Note: For this cut, the saw's blade guard cannot be used.)*

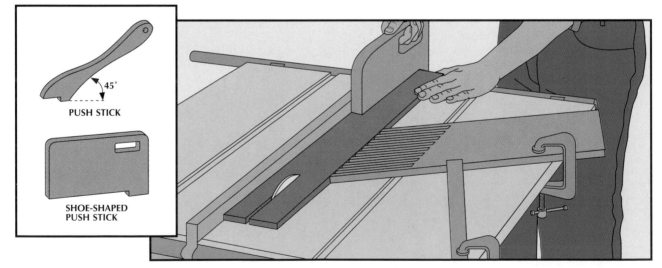

Shop-made push sticks.

Aids for feeding stock across saw and jointer tables can be made easily from scraps of $\frac{3}{4}$-inch plywood.

Cut out the forms with a saber saw or a band saw. Two common shapes are shown *(inset)*, but you can adapt the shape for the machine and job at hand. A push stick with an angle of 45 degrees is ideal for

most jobs on the table saw; on a radial-arm saw, a lower angle, with the handle closer to the table, allows the stick to slide under the arm. A rectangular shoe-shaped push stick allows you to apply greater downward pressure *(above)*, to keep the workpiece, particularly narrow stock, from rising up. *(Note: In this illustration, the blade guard has been removed for the sake of clarity.)*

A TILTING DRILL-PRESS TABLE

1. Constructing the table.

Equipped with a tilting table, a drill press can bore holes at any angle.

◆ Cut an 11- by 13-inch base and top from $\frac{3}{4}$-inch plywood, then join them with two 3-inch butt hinges.

◆ From 1-by-2s, cut two support brackets 10 inches long, then cut a $\frac{1}{2}$-inch slot from each one. Round the ends of the brackets so they won't protrude above the top.

◆ Fasten the support brackets to opposite sides of the top with $1\frac{1}{2}$-inch No. 8 wood screws, and to the base with $\frac{7}{16}$- by 2-inch hanger bolts *(photograph)*, washers, and wing nuts.

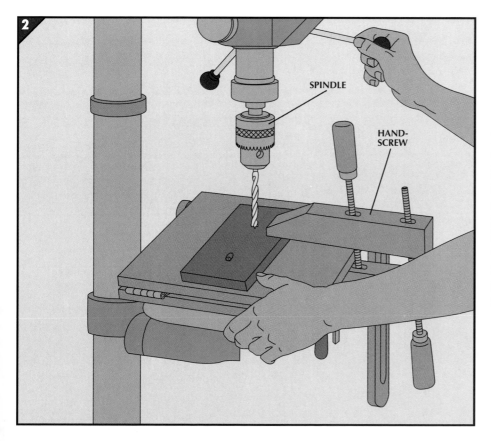

2. Boring angled holes.

◆ Loosen the wing nuts, raise the tilting table top to the desired angle, and tighten the nuts. Center the table under the spindle and clamp the base to the table with small quick-action bar clamps.

◆ For each hole, align the workpiece under the bit and clamp it to the jig—a wooden handscrew clamp is handy for this—then drill the hole *(left)*.

A Shop-Made Router Table

Easy and inexpensive to build, a router table transforms your router into a stationary tool for shaping edges and cutting grooves. The arrangement has advantages over hand-held routing. Feeding stock into the tool gives you greater control over the operation. Also, certain large router bits can be used only on a table-mounted router.

The table shown below features an ample top, an adjustable fence, a storage shelf, and a conveniently located on/off switch.

Design and Size: A typical table measures 25 inches by 40 inches, but you can vary the size to suit your needs. To ensure the table top is perfectly flat and even, prepare it by gluing together two sheets of $\frac{1}{2}$-inch medium-density fiberboard (MDF), which is flatter and more stable than plywood. You can cover the table top with plastic laminate for a smoother surface; sheathe the underside too so the top won't warp.

 TOOLS

Tape measure
Circular saw
Electric drill
  and assorted bits

Hammer
Screwdriver
Router
Awl
Saber saw
Jointer

 **MATERIALS**

Fiberboard ($\frac{1}{2}$")
2 x 4s
Plywood ($\frac{1}{2}$")
Wood glue
Wood screws ($\frac{3}{4}$", 2$\frac{1}{2}$", 3" No. 8)
Machine screws ($\frac{7}{8}$" No. 8)

Common nails (1$\frac{1}{2}$")
Angle irons (2")
Carriage bolts ($\frac{3}{8}$" x 3"), washers, and wing nuts
Polycarbonate sheet
Butt hinge
Switch-receptacle with electric cord

SAFETY TIPS

Wear goggles when nailing or when operating a power tool.

Anatomy of a router table.

A router table holds a router upside down with its bit protruding from a hole in the table top. The tool is screwed by its base to the underside of the table top. For the base, adapt the backboard-bench design shown on pages 71 and 72.

A miter slot routed across the top to one side of the bit allows a workpiece to be guided by a miter gauge for cross-grain routing. Make the slot the same width as your table saw's gauge. Combined with a clear plastic guard that offers protection from the bit, a fence is used for routing with the grain. The fence's slotted supports, with wing nuts that hold them in place, allow for quick adjustment of the fence.

A switched receptacle on one of the table legs saves the user from having to reach under the table for the router switch. The tool is plugged into the receptacle with its switch left on so it can be turned on and off with the receptacle's switch.

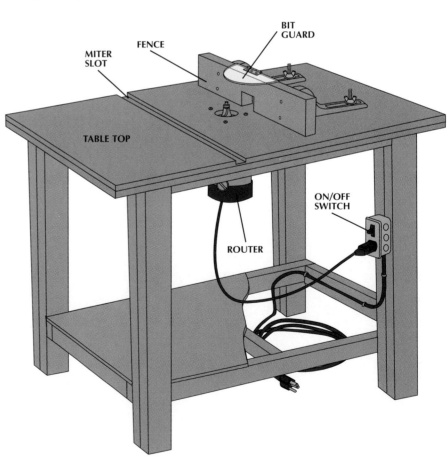

1. Preparing the top.

◆ Position the router on the underside of the table top and outline its base with a pencil.

◆ Rout a $\frac{1}{4}$-inch-deep recess within the outline. Separate the router body from its base, unscrew the thin plate under the base, and set the base in the recess.

◆ With an awl, mark the recess through the screw holes in the base *(right)*. Drill a hole for the screws at each mark and countersink them into the top surface of the table.

◆ With a spade bit or hole saw larger in diameter than your largest router bit, bore through the center of the recess.

◆ Set the router base in the recess, and fasten it to the table top with $\frac{7}{8}$-inch No. 8 machine screws.

◆ Secure the top to the table base with 2-inch angle irons and $\frac{3}{4}$-inch wood screws.

◆ Attach the router body to the base.

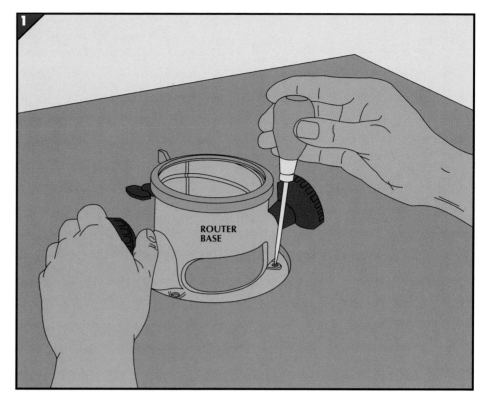

ROUTER BASE

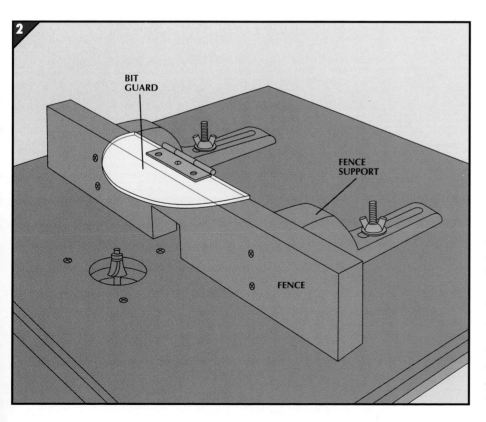

BIT GUARD

FENCE SUPPORT

FENCE

2. Adding the fence.

◆ Cut the fence and supports from 2-by-4s. With a saber saw, cut the supports to shape—wide at one end and narrow at the other—and cut $\frac{1}{2}$-inch slots in the narrow end.

◆ Run the face of the fence across a jointer to flatten it.

◆ Cut a notch from the fence's bottom edge to accommodate your largest bit.

◆ Drill countersunk pilot holes, then secure the fence to the supports with 3-inch No. 8 wood screws.

◆ Attach a clear semicircular piece of polycarbonate as a bit guard to the fence with a butt hinge so it can be raised out of the way if necessary.

◆ Set the fence assembly on the table about 1 inch from the bit opening. Drill a $\frac{3}{8}$-inch hole into the table top through the center of each slot. Fasten the fence to the table with 3-inch-long $\frac{3}{8}$-inch carriage bolts, washers, and wing nuts.

Certain jobs such as fixing a leaky faucet or patching wallboard cannot be undertaken in the shop. In such cases, you have to take the workshop to the job.

Tool and Material Carriers: A wooden toolbox *(below)* sized to accommodate the items you expect to carry is a worthwhile accessory. Rather than trying to transport all your tools in a single box, you may prefer to build two or more smaller carriers—one for all-purpose tools, another for electrical work, and a third to take to plumbing jobs.

A hardware organizer *(opposite, top)* is ideal for carrying small items such as nails, screws, bolts, nuts, and washers.

For toting cumbersome materials such as 4-by-8 sheets of plywood or wallboard, build a rope-handled carrier *(opposite, bottom)*.

Workstands: For jobs away from the shop that require a temporary workbench, you can set up and support a work surface with two folding sawhorses *(pages 96-97)*. Compact and simple to transport, these stands pass easily through doorways and, when not in use, hang almost flat against the shop wall.

 TOOLS

Tape measure
Circular saw
Electric drill
Screwdriver
Pliers
Saber saw
Protractor
T-bevel
Handsaw
Wood chisel
Mallet
Hammer

 **MATERIALS**

1 x 3s
2 x 4s
Plywood ($\frac{1}{2}$")
Wood dowel ($\frac{7}{8}$")
Wood glue
Cotter pins
Wood screws (1", $1\frac{1}{4}$", No. 6; $1\frac{1}{4}$", 3" No. 8)
Carriage bolts ($\frac{3}{8}$" x $2\frac{1}{2}$", 5"), washers, nuts, and wing nuts
Butt hinges (3")
Rope
Plastic pipe

SAFETY TIPS

Wear goggles when nailing or when operating a power tool.

HOMEMADE CARRIERS FOR TOOLS AND MATERIALS

Building an open toolbox.
◆ From $\frac{1}{2}$-inch plywood, cut the sides, end panels, and bottom pieces of the box, sized to accommodate your tool collection. The sides can typically be about 8 inches high and the ends high enough to position the handle above the tools.
◆ Drill $\frac{7}{8}$-inch holes for the handle near the top of the end panels, stacked so the holes will line up.
◆ Fasten the pieces together with glue and $1\frac{1}{4}$-inch No. 6 wood screws.
◆ Add tool-holding accessories such as a slotted saw holder, screwed to the bottom of the box, and a tool rack fastened in a corner.
◆ For the handle, drill a hole through a length of $\frac{7}{8}$-inch wood dowel near each end and slide it through the holes in the end panels. To hold the handle in place, insert cotter pins in the holes and bend back their ends.

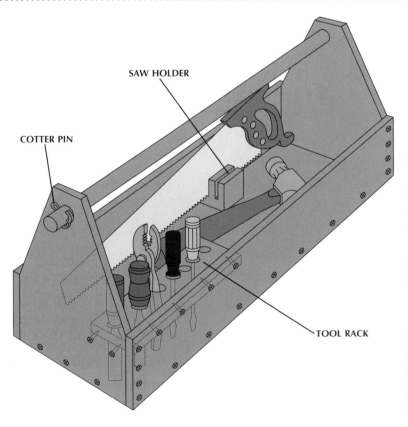

SAW HOLDER

COTTER PIN

TOOL RACK

Keeping fasteners organized.

◆ Design a box large enough to hold the planned contents and partitions, then cut the pieces for the sides, bottom, and dividers from $\frac{1}{2}$-inch plywood.

◆ With a saber saw, cut a handhold in the middle divider.

◆ With glue and 1-inch No. 6 wood screws, fasten the sides to the bottom, and individual dividers to the long middle divider. Then fasten the entire divider assembly to the box.

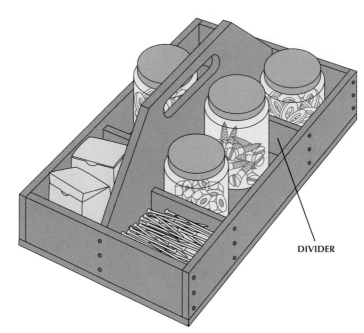

DIVIDER

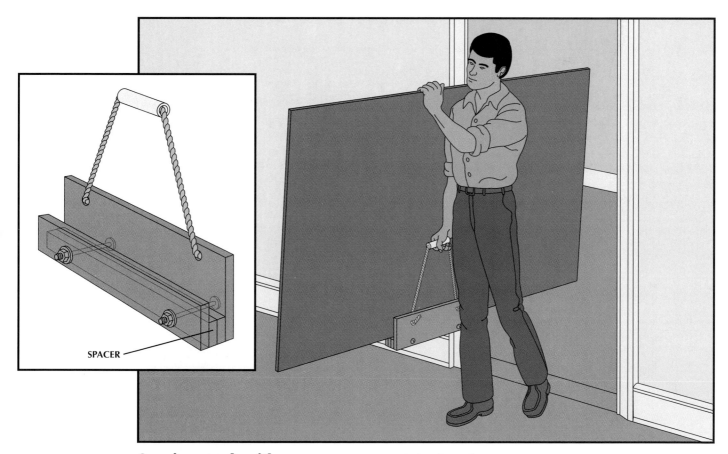

SPACER

Carrying panels with ease.

◆ From $\frac{1}{2}$-inch plywood, cut two 16-inch-long pieces for the sides of the carrier; make one 2 inches high and the other 4 inches high. For the spacer, cut two pieces of plywood 1 inch high and glue them together face to face.

◆ Sandwich the spacer between the sides; glue the pieces together, then drill two $\frac{3}{8}$-inch holes through all three, and join them with $\frac{3}{8}$- by $2\frac{1}{2}$-inch carriage bolts.

◆ Bore two holes along the upper edge of the high side for a rope handle. Thread a short length of plastic pipe or garden hose over the rope as a hand grip, and knot the rope against the carrier. The knot may be untied and adjusted to suit the height of the person carrying the panel.

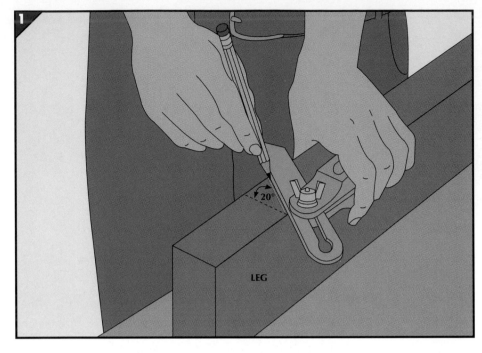

1. Cutting the legs.

If you will be using a circular saw, mark two lines across the face of each 2-by-4 leg, 2 feet apart, tilt the saw's base plate to 20 degrees, and cut the legs at the lines.

◆ If you're using a handsaw, first set the blade of a T-bevel to 20 degrees with a protractor and hold the blade against a leg to mark one end *(left)*.
◆ Mark the opposite end with a parallel line 24 inches away.
◆ To guide the blade as you cut the angled ends, extend both lines completely around the leg, marking straight lines across the faces of the 2-by-4 and angled lines on the edge.
◆ Cut the leg, then use it as a pattern for sawing the other three.

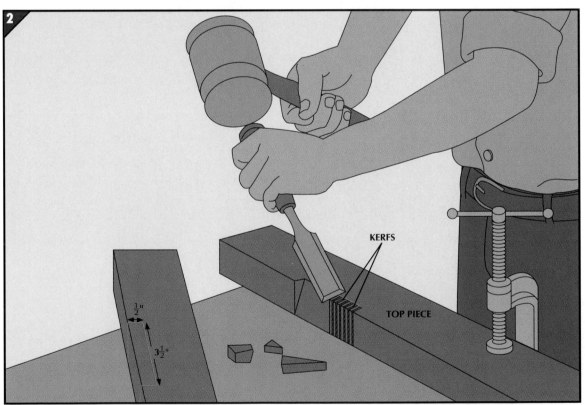

2. Notching the top pieces.

◆ Cut two 30-inch-long 2-by-4s for the top.
◆ Along one edge of each piece, mark a $3\frac{1}{2}$-inch-wide notch for the legs 4 inches from each end. Also mark a line on the face of the board, inset $\frac{1}{2}$ inch from the edge to define the angle of the notch.
◆ With a handsaw, cut kerfs at $\frac{1}{4}$-inch intervals across the notch outline. Clear out the bulk of the waste with a chisel and mallet, keeping the bevel of the chisel toward the waste *(above)*. To clean up the notch, move the chisel with hand pressure only.
◆ To attach each leg, hold it in its notch flush with the surface of a top piece, drill pilot holes for three 3-inch No. 8 wood screws, then secure the leg to the top.

3. Hinging the top.

◆ Butt the top pieces against each other upside down and hold them together temporarily with nails and a piece of scrap wood.

◆ Place two 3-inch butt hinges across the joint between the top pieces about 6 inches from the ends; mark the holes, drill a pilot hole at each mark, and fasten the hinges with $1\frac{1}{4}$-inch screws *(right)*.

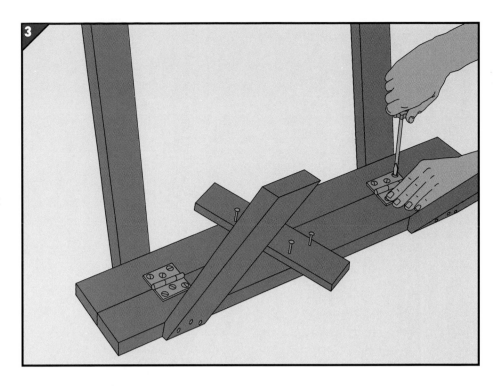

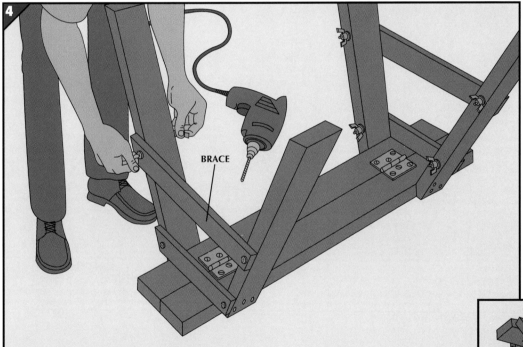

4. Bolting braces to the legs.

◆ For each top brace, hold a 1-by-3 across a pair of legs and butted against the underside of the top, and mark the outside edge of the legs on the 1-by-3. Mark bottom braces 10 inches lower down the legs. Saw the braces to length.

◆ Tack the upper braces to the legs and drill $\frac{3}{8}$-inch clearance holes through the braces and legs. Remove the nails and attach the braces with

5-inch carriage bolts, washers, and wing nuts.

◆ Remove the scrap wood, and secure the lower braces the same way *(above)*.

To fold the sawhorse for transport or storage *(inset)*, remove one bolt from each brace and let the braces hang free; the hinges under the top will let the legs collapse. Store the bolts you removed in the legs.

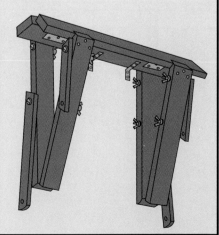

A Bench for Metalworking

Anyone whose specialty is metalworking will appreciate the practical island-style bench pictured below and opposite. Weighted at the base, it is small enough to allow you to circle the work, approaching it from any angle. The durable steel-plate top is absolutely flat—an advantage if your work includes aligning metal seams. Although the base and top together weigh more than 400 pounds, the bench can be tipped onto a dolly and moved fairly easily.

Buying and Preparing the Metal: Purchase an empty 55-gallon drum and have a metalworking shop trim it down, or do the job yourself with a hacksaw. Both the steel plate for the top and the angle irons for the legs are available at metal-products shops. Choose ungalvanized steel for the top, to reduce glare.

Most metal shops will cut and drill holes in the metal parts to your specifications *(below)*, and can shape a square steel plate into a round disk. You can cut costs by leaving the top square, but you may find that the sharp corners are a hazard.

 TOOLS

Saber saw
Wrench
Carpenter's square

C-clamps
Electric drill
Screwdriver
Metalworking vise

 **MATERIALS**

Plywood (1")
Concrete
2 x 4s
Angle irons
  ($\frac{1}{4}$" x 2" x 2")

Lag screws ($\frac{3}{8}$" x 1"),
  washers
Machine bolts ($\frac{3}{8}$" x 1"),
  lock washers, and nuts
Drum (55-gallon)
Steel plate ($\frac{1}{4}$")
Wood screws (1" No. 8)

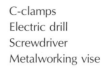 **SAFETY TIPS**

Wear goggles when hammering or when using power tools. Put on gloves and goggles to mix and pour concrete.

A metalworking bench.

For the table top, a sheet of 1-inch plywood cut 32 inches in diameter has a matching $\frac{1}{4}$-inch steel plate attached to it with screws running through eight countersunk holes, evenly spaced, about 2 inches from the edge. Each side of the top is supported by a leg assembly that includes a 21-inch rail and two 24-inch legs made of $\frac{1}{4}$- by 2- by 2-inch angle iron. The top flanges of the rails are bolted to the plywood with three lag screws running through holes 8 inches apart. The legs are fastened to the vertical flanges of the rails, $3\frac{1}{2}$ inches from each end, with machine bolts running through a hole in the top of each leg. A 55-gallon drum, cut to a height of 16 inches, is filled with approximately 4 cubic feet of concrete, and the legs are sunk in the concrete so the table height falls at knuckle level when the owner is standing next to it with loosely hanging arms. A metalworking vise is fastened to the top with machine bolts and nuts.

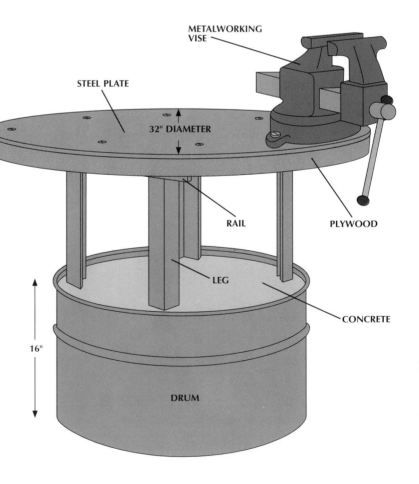

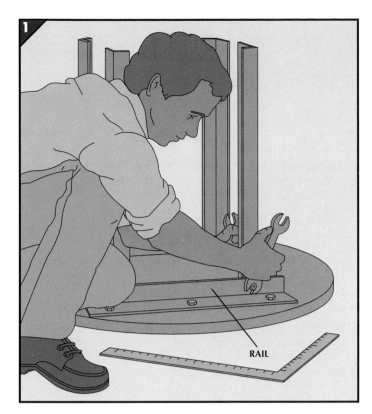

RAIL

1. Assembling the benchtop.

◆ With a saber saw, cut a piece of 1-inch plywood into a circle 32 inches in diameter.

◆ Set the rails on the underside of the top, placing them parallel and 16 inches apart, with their vertical flanges inward. Mark the holes in the rails and drill pilot holes into the top, then anchor the rails to the top with $\frac{3}{8}$- by 1-inch lag screws.

◆ Bolt the legs to the rails with $\frac{3}{8}$- by 1-inch machine bolts, placing a lock washer behind each nut. Check with a square that the legs are perpendicular to the top, then tighten the fasteners (left).

CHOOSING A METALWORKING VISE

A solid vise is indispensable for metal-working. One with jaws that open to about 5 inches works well for most home workshop needs. Look for a vise with a swivel base and replace-able jaw plates. The model shown here has an integral anvil next to the right-hand jaw for shaping metal.

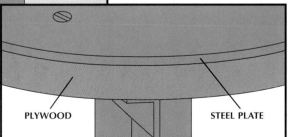

PLYWOOD   STEEL PLATE

2. Embedding the legs in the base.

◆ Clamp a 24-inch-long 2-by-4 across each pair of legs about one-third from their bottom ends.

◆ Fill the base with concrete and sink the legs into it, letting the 2-by-4s rest on the rim.

◆ Loosen the clamps and adjust the position of the legs so the top is level and at the desired height (above).

◆ Allow the concrete to set for 48 hours, then remove the clamps and 2-by-4s.

◆ Set the steel plate on the top, drill pilot holes in the plywood through the holes in the plate, then attach the plate with 1-inch No. 8 wood screws, driving them so the heads lie flush with the plate (inset).

A Booth for Spray Painting

The most effective way to apply a finish smoothly and evenly is by spraying it. However, the process releases toxic and sometimes flammable substances into the air. A properly constructed spray booth *(below)* will contain the spray and vent it to the outdoors.

A Three-Sided Room: An effective spray booth is typically designed as an open-ended rectangle equipped with a powerful, specially designed exhaust fan at the inside end. The fan draws fumes through a filter and sends them outside; the filter traps drifting spray. Before committing yourself to a design, check local codes; also check how a spray booth will affect your home insurance. The size of the booth and the fan can vary, but always locate them at least 20 feet away from any open flame such as a furnace or the pilot light of a water heater. Situate the booth so you can vent the fan through a window opening in an exterior wall, with no buildings, bushes, or other barriers on the outside closer than 6 feet.

Expelling Bad Air: The exhaust fan and its filter are the most important components of the booth. Choose a fan designed especially for spray booths, with a motor and drive belt shielded from the air passing through the fan duct. To cover the opening in the vent wall, buy a special paint-arrester filter. Your fan supplier will have a round-to-square adapter duct to connect the square filter to the round fan.

 **TOOLS**

Tape measure
Circular saw
Saber saw
Electric drill
Plumb bob
Carpenter's square
Hammer
Carpenter's level
Screwdriver
Caulking gun

 **MATERIALS**

Plywood ($\frac{3}{4}$")
2 x 4s
Common nails (3", $3\frac{1}{2}$")
Wood screws ($\frac{3}{4}$", 2" No. 8)
Masonry nails (3")
Exhaust fan
Fan shutter
Duct adapter
Filter frame and filters
Fireproof wallboard
Wallboard installation materials
Caulk

 SAFETY TIPS

Wear goggles when nailing, operating power tools, or working with finishes and other chemicals. When spraying a finish, don a dual-cartridge respirator.

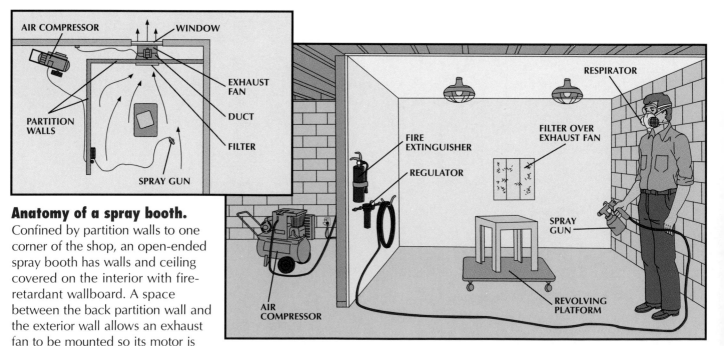

Anatomy of a spray booth.
Confined by partition walls to one corner of the shop, an open-ended spray booth has walls and ceiling covered on the interior with fire-retardant wallboard. A space between the back partition wall and the exterior wall allows an exhaust fan to be mounted so its motor is isolated from the booth *(inset)*. The air compressor is positioned outside the booth. Explosion-proof light sockets masked by wire or plastic baskets provide overhead lighting, and all electrical switches and outlets are mounted outside the booth. A fire extinguisher is placed on the wall near the opening. The revolving platform at the center of the booth allows the user to remain upwind of the spray.

BUILDING THE SPRAY BOOTH

1. Installing the exhaust fan.

◆ Cut a backer board of $\frac{3}{4}$-inch plywood to fit the window opening. With a saber saw, cut a hole in the backing to match the opening in the fan casing.

◆ Fasten a 2-by-4 mounting block with 3-inch common nails to the window sill flush with the outside edge of the window stool.

◆ Position the fan's mounting flange against the backer board *(right),* then secure it with $\frac{3}{4}$-inch No. 8 wood screws.

◆ To attach the backer board to the mounting block and to the window sash, drill pilot holes, then fasten it with 2-inch wood screws.

◆ Insert the round end of the round-to-square duct adapter into the fan casing, and install a fan shutter outside the window to keep out cold air and rain.

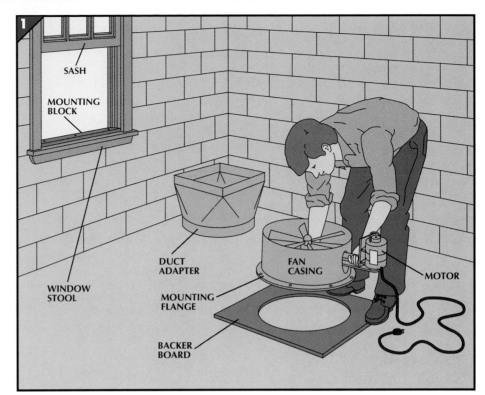

SASH
MOUNTING BLOCK
DUCT ADAPTER
FAN CASING
MOTOR
WINDOW STOOL
MOUNTING FLANGE
BACKER BOARD

2. Planning the partition walls.

◆ Place the fan assembly in the window, then drop a plumb bob from the duct adapter to the floor 2 inches from the front edge of the duct; mark the point where the plumb bob meets the floor *(left).*

◆ Repeat the measurement on the other side of the adapter, then draw a line connecting the two points and extend it the desired length of the vent wall. Checking with a carpenter's square, draw a second line perpendicular to the first to mark the side wall.

◆ Cut two 2-by-4s to serve as top and sole plates for the vent wall and lay them side by side on the floor.

◆ On the plates, outline two 2-by-4 studs to frame the fan duct at each plumb-bob mark on the floor *(inset).* Mark off additional stud positions along the plates at 16-inch intervals.

◆ Cut top and sole plates for the marked side wall, and outline stud positions at 16-inch intervals along the boards. Then cut 2-by-4 studs for the vent and side walls 3 inches shorter than the floor-to-ceiling height.

FAN-DUCT MARK

SOLE PLATE

TOP PLATE

END STUD

SECOND STUD

NAILING BLOCK

3. Raising the partition walls.

◆ With $3\frac{1}{2}$-inch nails, fasten the studs to the top plate of the vent wall at the marked outlines, driving two nails into each stud *(above)*.

◆ Place the outside edge of the vent wall's sole plate along the line on the floor and nail it in place with 3-inch masonry nails.

◆ Raise the top-plate-and-stud assembly into position, then nail the top plate to the ceiling joists and toenail the bottoms of the studs to the sole plate

at the marked outlines. Check with a level as you go to keep the wall plumb.

◆ Assemble the side partition wall in the same way. At the end that will connect to the vent wall, fasten 2-by-4 nailing blocks at the top, middle, and bottom of the outside stud, then fasten a second stud to the blocks *(inset)*.

◆ When the side wall is in place, nail the end stud of the vent wall to the nailing blocks of the side wall.

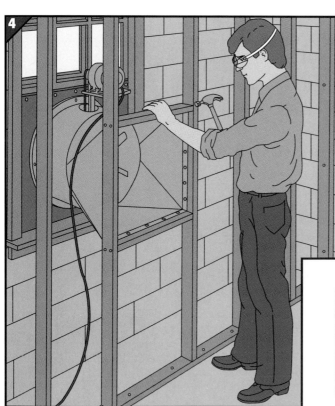

4. Completing the walls and fan assembly.

◆ Frame the top and bottom of the fan duct with 2-by-4s, nailing them into place between studs *(left)*. Drill clearance holes through the duct's flange and fasten it to the frame with $\frac{3}{4}$-inch wood screws.

◆ Install fire-retardant wallboard on the inside of the partition walls and over other combustible surfaces, such as exposed ceiling joists. Caulk the joints between wallboard panels to make them airtight.

◆ To install the fan's filter assembly *(inset)*, screw the metal frame for the filter into the opening in the vent wall flush with the inside edges of the framing studs. Then snap the filter grid into the filter frame, insert the filter material, and snap in the two retainer rods that hold the material in place.

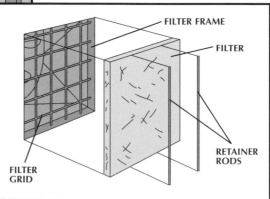

FILTER FRAME

FILTER

RETAINER RODS

FILTER GRID

A Space-Efficient Tool Turret

Turntables have been used for years in homes and industry to increase the accessibility of work and storage areas. Here, a round platform 3 feet in diameter is mounted on a turntable to transform a bench corner into a work center and storage site for three small power tools—a grinder, a drill stand holding a portable electric drill, and a scroll saw. Other tools may be substituted for these three if they can be used in tight quarters and their weight is evenly distributed around the platform. Such an arrangement is most useful when it is positioned in the corner of either an L-shaped bench or a counter built against adjoining walls.

The platform is set on a lazy Susan—consisting of two interlocking disks sandwiching a ring of ball bearings—rated to carry a load of up to 1000 pounds. The table can be locked in any of three positions with a wood dowel set into a hole drilled through the platform.

 TOOLS

Saber saw
Electric drill
Counterbore bit
Screwdriver

 **MATERIALS**

Plywood ($\frac{3}{4}$")
Heavy-duty lazy Susan and flat-head stove bolts
Wood screws (1" No. 8)
Dowel ($\frac{1}{2}$")

SAFETY TIPS

Wear goggles when operating power tools.

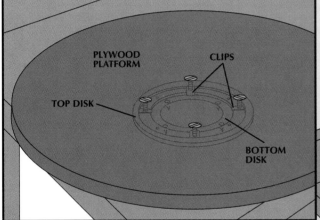

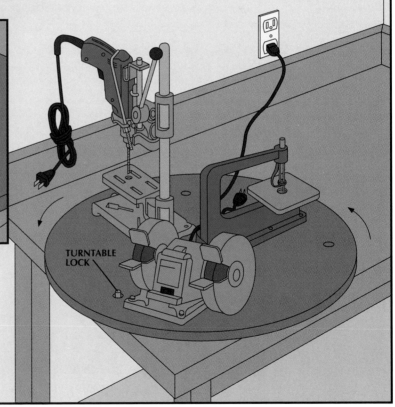

Making a tool turntable.

◆ With a pencil tied to a string, mark a 36-inch-diameter circle on a piece of $\frac{3}{4}$-inch plywood and cut it with a saber saw.
◆ Turn the plywood over and mark the holes of the lazy Susan's top disk, then drill a $\frac{1}{4}$-inch hole at each mark. Set the plywood right-side up and countersink the drilled holes.
◆ Fasten the bottom disk of the lazy Susan to the workbench with 1-inch No. 8 wood screws.
◆ Set the plywood on top of the lazy Susan and thread flat-head stove bolts through the holes to engage the clips that serve as nuts for the bolts *(inset)*.
◆ For locking the turntable in position, drill three $\frac{1}{2}$-inch holes through the turntable 4 inches from the edge and evenly spaced around the platform. At one of the holes continue drilling into the

workbench about 1 inch, then cut a $\frac{1}{2}$-inch dowel so it will protrude 1 inch above the surface of the platform when inserted into the hole.
◆ Screw the tools to the turntable.
◆ If the table seems unsteady, slide blocks of wood under the plywood and clamp them to the workbench.

Keeping a Workshop Organized

A neat and uncluttered workshop, where tools, hardware, and materials are sorted and stored in an organized fashion, will make your work easier, safer, and more enjoyable. This chapter shows you how to build and set up a range of storage aids, as well as how to keep dust and debris under control.

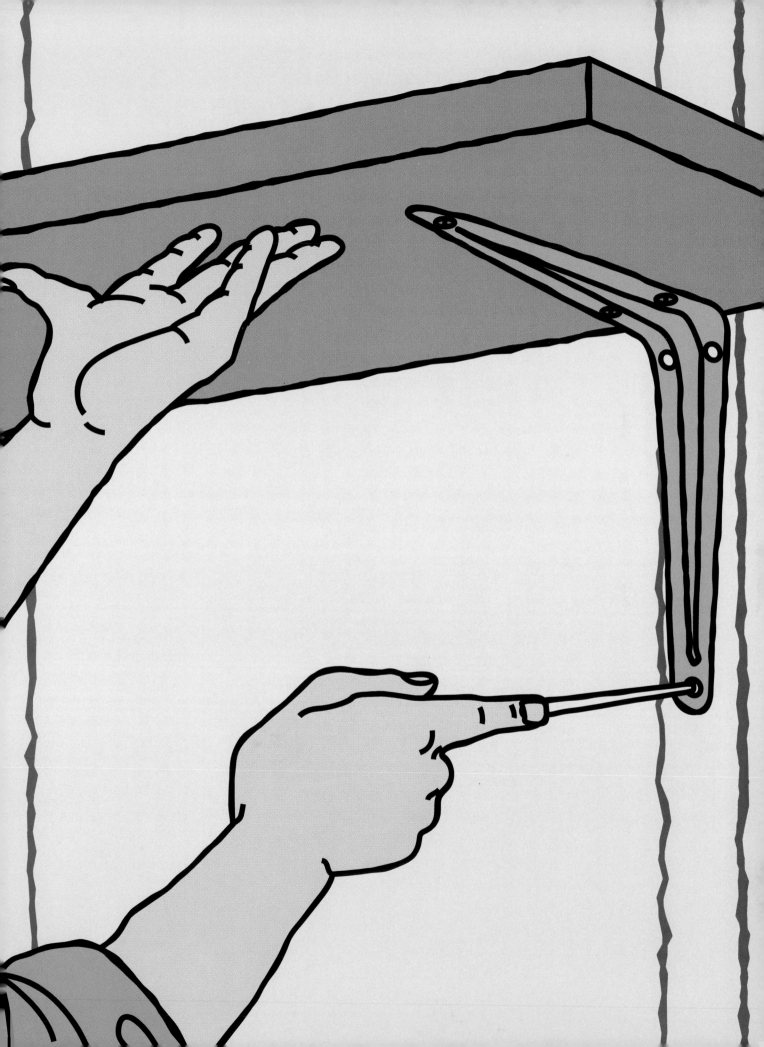

Storage in the Workshop

Storing tools and materials so they remain in good condition and are easily accessible is essential for a smoothly running shop. Careful planning will allow you to make the most efficient use of the space you have.

Simple Hangers: An easy way to hang tools and supplies is to drive 2½-inch finishing nails into wall-mounted plywood. To protect fine tools from scratches, use wooden dowel pegs instead of nails.

Versatile Pegboard: Perforated tempered hardboard—known as pegboard (*opposite*)—coupled with a variety of metal and plastic hangers can transform a wall, the inside of a door, or the side of a table into efficient storage surfaces. A ⅛-inch-thick sheet will hold small hand tools such as screwdrivers, pliers, and wrenches; ¼-inch is best for heavier items.

Drawers: Shallow drawers hung beneath the workbench (*pages 108-110*) are convenient for storing small tools. They can also be divided into compartments tailored to suit their contents.

 TOOLS

Tape measure	Router and bits
Circular saw	(straight, rabbeting)
Hammer	Table saw
Electric drill	C-clamps
Counterbore bit	Bar clamps
Screwdriver	Mallet
Straightedge	Backsaw
	Sanding block
	Table saw

 **MATERIALS**

Pegboard	Brads (1")
and hangers	Wood screws (2"
1 x 2s	No. 6; 1" No. 8)
1 x 4s	Wood glue
Plywood (¼")	Dowel (¼")
Common nails (2")	Sandpaper
	(medium grade)
	Paraffin

 **SAFETY TIPS**

Wear goggles when nailing or operating power tools.

Storing tools efficiently.
This workshop combines several practical tool-storage systems. Pegboard above the workbench and on the sides of the bench and table saw, and racks made of dowels in plywood strips fastened to wall studs, store hand tools within easy reach. Wall shelves display supplies, and drawers hung beneath the workbench keep small items confined. The notched rack against the wall holds bar clamps, and a wooden cleat just above the workbench stores spring clamps and C-clamps; even the joists are utilized. A lockable cabinet on casters safeguards power tools such as drills and routers, and provides an extra work surface.

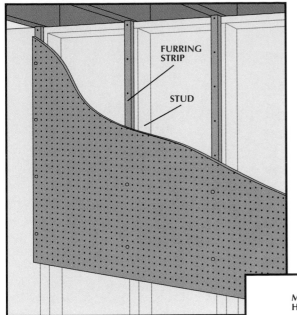

FURRING STRIP

STUD

Mounting pegboard.

In a typical installation *(left)*, 1-by-2 furring strips hold the pegboard $\frac{3}{4}$ inch from the wall to allow space for the backs of the hangers. The furring strips are nailed to wall studs with 2-inch common nails, then 1-inch No. 8 wood screws and washers at 6-inch intervals fasten the board to the furring strips.

On a concrete-block wall, use masonry nails and construction adhesive to fasten the furring strips to the blocks.

Hangers for pegboard.

A wide variety of pegboard hangers is available; some common types are shown at right. Multiple hangers hold screwdrivers and pliers. Clamp hangers offer firm support for chisels and other round-handled tools. The versatile U-hook is suitable for tools with straps, holes, or loop-shaped handles; the type with an extra tip on the back *(inset)* keeps the hook from swiveling. Plate hangers support flat-bottomed tools such as sharpening stones. A single-loop hanger is convenient for clamps, a hand drill, or handsaw. A double hanger is ideal for a hammer.

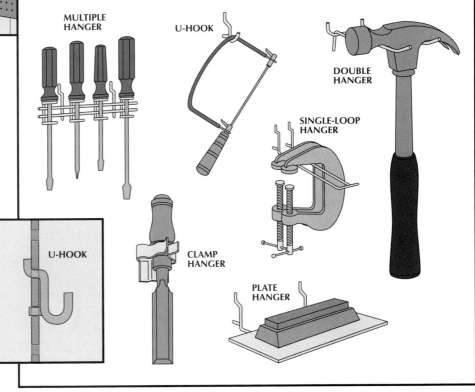

MULTIPLE HANGER

U-HOOK

DOUBLE HANGER

SINGLE-LOOP HANGER

U-HOOK

CLAMP HANGER

PLATE HANGER

TRICKS OF THE TRADE

Anchoring Hangers

To prevent pegboard hangers from falling off the board when you remove a tool, place a large drop of hot glue on each hanger hook just before slipping it in place. If you need to subsequently reposition a hanger, hold a heat gun against the pegboard for a few seconds to soften the glue.

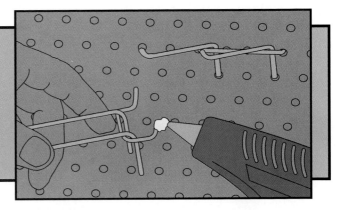

A DRAWER HUNG UNDERNEATH A WORKTABLE

Anatomy of a drawer.

This drawer is a simple box with the front, back, and sides cut from a 1-by-4, and the bottom made from $\frac{1}{4}$-inch plywood. Dimensions depend on your needs and on the size of worktable to which the drawer will be attached, but certain features are shared by all sizes.

The drawer front has rabbets cut into both ends to accommodate the sides. The drawer back, cut $\frac{3}{4}$ inch narrower than the front, fits into dadoes cut into each side piece $\frac{1}{2}$ inch from the end. The plywood bottom, $\frac{5}{8}$ inch longer and wider than the inside dimensions of the drawer, is held in a dado cut near the bottom edges of the 1-by-4s.

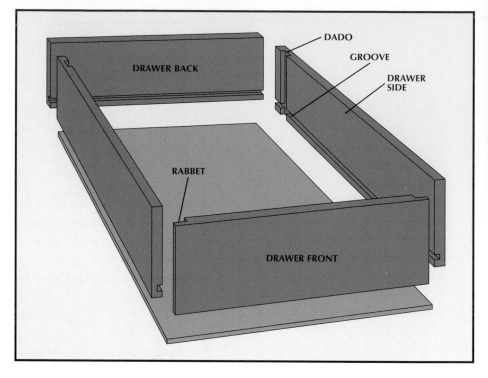

1. Cutting the dadoes and rabbets.

◆ On a 1-by-4 board as long as the combined lengths of the drawer front, back, and sides, draw lines $\frac{3}{8}$ and $\frac{5}{8}$ inch from one edge.

◆ Butt a $\frac{3}{4}$-inch-thick support board against the 1-by-4, and set a straight-edged cutting guide on top of the support board.

◆ Install a $\frac{1}{4}$-inch straight bit (photograph) in a router. With the router bit aligned between the groove lines, butt the cutting guide against the tool's base, then clamp it in place.

◆ Rout a $\frac{1}{4}$-inch groove along the length of the 1-by-4 (left), moving the clamp out of the way if necessary.

◆ Mark the lengths of the front, back, and sides on the board (inset), then cut them.

◆ With a $\frac{3}{4}$-inch straight bit, rout a $\frac{3}{8}$-inch-deep dado into each side piece, $\frac{1}{2}$-inch from the end.

◆ Rout a $\frac{9}{16}$-inch-deep rabbet into the ends of the drawer front.

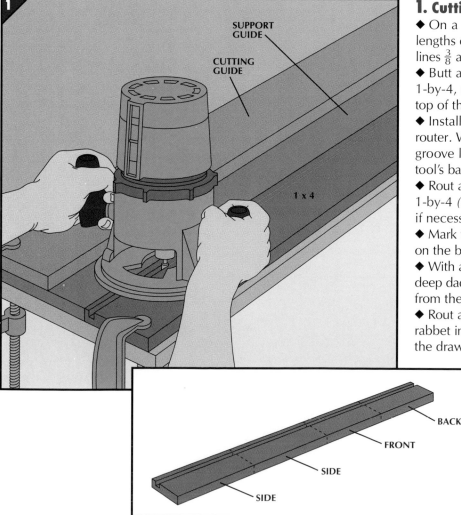

2. Assembling the drawer.

◆ Spread wood glue in the vertical dadoes in the side pieces and place the back of the drawer into them. Secure the assembly with a bar clamp.

◆ Cut the drawer bottom $\frac{5}{8}$ inch longer and wider than the inside measurements of the drawer.

◆ Set the drawer on its back and slide the bottom into its horizontal dadoes *(right)*; do not glue the bottom in place.

◆ Spread glue in the rabbets in the drawer front, position the front against the sides and bottom, then clamp it in place.

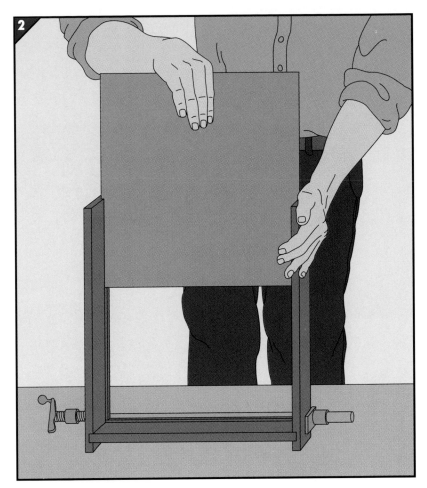

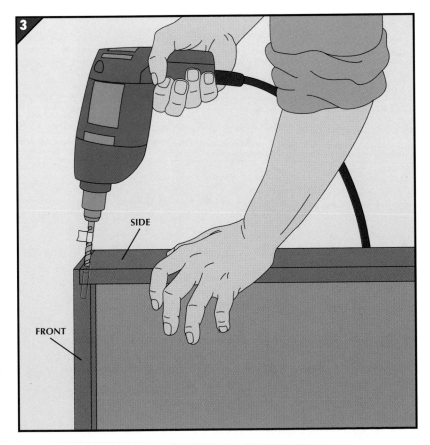

3. Doweling the drawer front.

◆ Wrap a piece of masking tape as a depth gauge around a $\frac{1}{4}$-inch drill bit $1\frac{1}{4}$ inches from the end.

◆ Holding the bit about $\frac{1}{2}$ inch from the top edge of the drawer side and $\frac{1}{2}$ inch from the front edge, bore a hole at a slight angle through the side into the front *(left)*. To avoid drilling through the drawer front, stop when the masking-tape gauge contacts the wood. Make another hole at the bottom edge of the drawer side and two more through the opposite side.

◆ Cut four pieces of $\frac{1}{4}$-inch dowel about $1\frac{1}{2}$ inches long. Squirt glue in the holes and tap the dowels in with a mallet. Cut off the ends of the dowels with a backsaw, then use medium-grade sandpaper to sand them flush with the drawer sides.

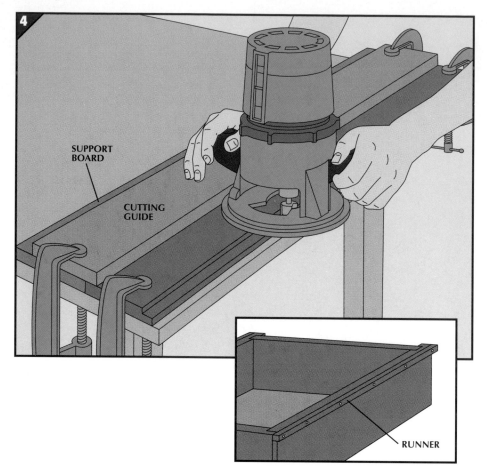

SUPPORT BOARD

CUTTING GUIDE

RUNNER

4. Cutting the drawer guides.

Runners fastened to the drawer sides along their top edges fit into guides attached to the underside of the worktable, enabling the drawer to be slid in and out.

◆ For each guide, cut a 1-by-4 to the width of the worktable.

◆ Place a 1-inch-thick support board beside the 1-by-4. Fit a $\frac{3}{4}$-inch straight bit *(photograph)* into the router, position a cutting guide so the bit will cut a $\frac{3}{8}$-inch-wide, $\frac{3}{8}$-inch-deep rabbet in the 1-by-4's edge. Clamp the boards and cutting guide to the work surface, then rout the rabbet *(left)*, moving the clamp out of the way if necessary.

◆ Cut the 1-by-4 in half and rip it $1\frac{1}{2}$ inches wide.

◆ To make runners, rip a length of 1-by stock $\frac{3}{8}$ inch thick and wide on a table saw. Fasten the runners to the drawer sides with glue and 1-inch brads *(inset)*.

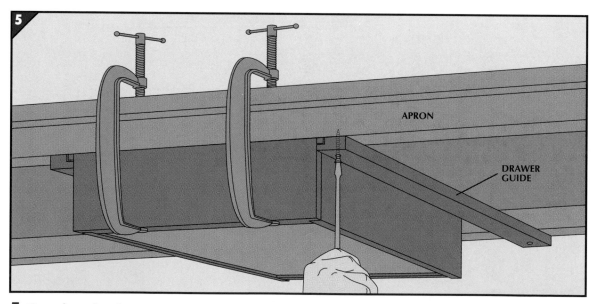

APRON

DRAWER GUIDE

5. Hanging the drawer.

◆ Holding the wide edge of a drawer guide against the underside of the table's aprons, drill countersunk clearance holes for 2-inch No. 6 wood screws through it at the center of each apron. Repeat for the other guide.

◆ Clamp the drawer in its closed position under the table. Holding one drawer guide over a runner with a small gap between the guide and runner, drill pilot holes up into the aprons, through the holes in the guide. Then do the same with the other guide.

◆ Fasten the guides to the table *(above)*.

◆ Screw a small block of wood to the back of each guide to stop the drawer from sliding too far under the bench.

◆ Sand the adjoining surfaces of the runners and tracks. Lubricate the guides with paraffin so the drawer will slide smoothly.

One of the most versatile storage aids is a cabinet mounted on casters, which can be rolled from one work area to another. With a lockable door, it can be used to safeguard tools or materials. Its adjustable shelves extend its storage capability, and it can double as an extra work surface.

Sizing the Cabinet: Make the length, width, and depth of the cabinet to suit the bulk and number of items you plan to store in it. For the height, determine how you want to use the cabinet when it is stationary; as an assembly table it should be shorter than an auxiliary workbench—shorter still if you want to store the cabinet under a table when it is not in use.

Materials: For a good compromise between durability and economy, use interior-grade plywood for all but the back of the cabinet, which can be made of plywood or hardboard. Mount the cabinet on locking casters—they'll keep the cabinet immobilized when necessary. For loads up to 35 pounds, install 3-inch casters; for heavier loads, choose 4-inch casters.

TOOLS

Tape measure	Hammer
Circular saw	Mallet
Electric drill	Carpenter's
C-clamps	square
Bar clamps	Wood chisel
Router and bits	Awl
(straight,	Screwdriver
rabbeting)	

MATERIALS

Plywood ($\frac{1}{4}$", $\frac{3}{4}$")
Shelf supports
Wood glue
Offset hinges ($\frac{3}{4}$")
Wood screws ($\frac{3}{4}$"
   No. 8)
Finishing nails
   (1", $2\frac{1}{4}$")
Magnetic catch
Casters (swivel-
   type, locking)

SAFETY TIPS

Wear goggles when nailing or when operating power tools.

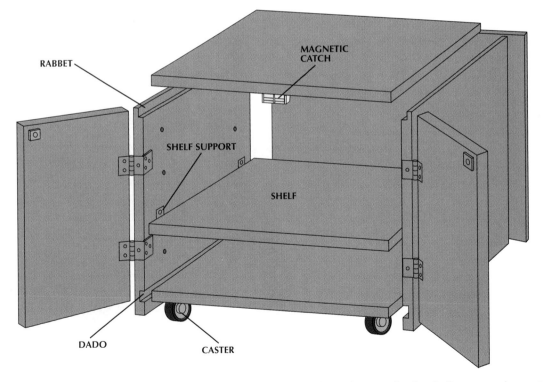

RABBET

MAGNETIC CATCH

SHELF SUPPORT

SHELF

DADO   CASTER

Planning the cabinet.

The sides, top, bottom, shelf, and doors of this cabinet are all made of $\frac{3}{4}$-inch interior-grade plywood; the back is cut from $\frac{1}{4}$-inch plywood. The width of the top is $\frac{3}{4}$ inch shorter than the overall width of the cabinet so it can fit into rabbets cut in the tops of the sides. The bottom, cut to the same dimensions as the top, fits into dadoes 2 inches from the bottom of the cabinet. The back fits squarely against the top, sides, and bottom.

Shelf supports fit into holes drilled in the sides. The doors are fastened to the cabinet sides with offset hinges; tool racks can be added to the inside of the doors, as shown on page 106. Magnetic catches keep the doors closed. The cabinet rides on swiveling casters.

PUTTING THE PIECES TOGETHER

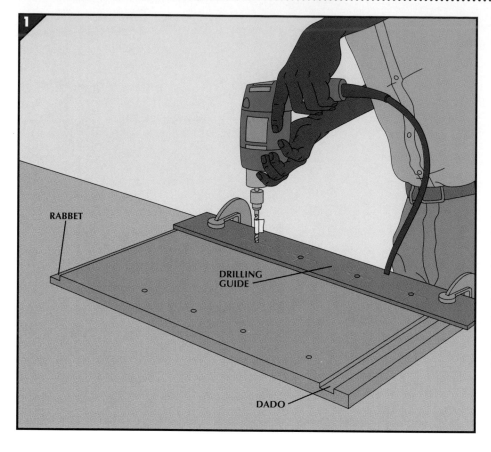

RABBET

DRILLING GUIDE

DADO

1. Preparing the cabinet parts.

◆ Cut $\frac{3}{4}$-inch plywood to size for the top, bottom, and sides.

◆ In each of the cabinet sides, rout a $\frac{3}{4}$-inch-wide, $\frac{3}{8}$-inch-deep rabbet along the top edge, and a dado the same size 1 inch from the bottom edge using the techniques on page 108, Step 1.

◆ Make a guide to drill the shelf support holes: In a board, drill holes that will accommodate the shelf supports at the desired intervals. Start the holes 5 inches from one end of the board and offset them from the edge by $1\frac{1}{2}$ inches.

◆ Align the guide with the cabinet side and bottom and clamp it in place.

◆ For a depth stop, wrap masking tape around the bit $\frac{5}{8}$ inch from the tip. Drill the holes, stopping when the masking tape reaches the wood, then drill the holes on the other side *(left)*.

2. Assembling the cabinet.

◆ Apply wood glue to the dadoes and rabbets in the cabinet sides and fit the top and bottom in place; checking that the cabinet is square with a carpenter's square, secure the panels together with bar or pipe clamps and $2\frac{1}{4}$-inch finishing nails driven every 6 inches along the joints.

◆ Cut the back of the cabinet from $\frac{1}{4}$-inch plywood or hardboard.

◆ Attach the back to the assembly with 1-inch finishing nails *(right)*.

◆ To size the doors, measure the width of the cabinet, then the height from the lower edge of the bottom piece to the top; cut a piece of $\frac{3}{4}$-inch plywood to these dimensions. Cut the piece in half to create two doors—the kerf left by the saw blade will provide clearance between the doors.

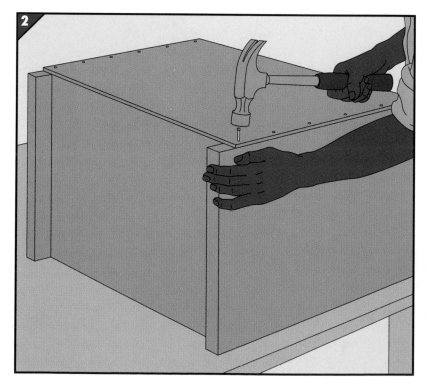

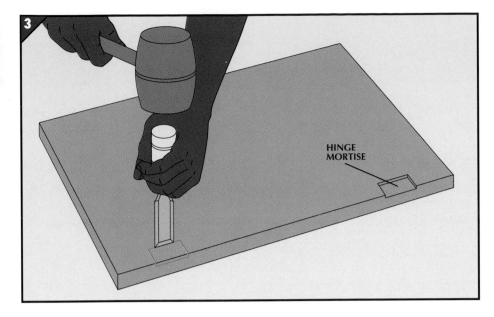

3. Chiseling the hinge mortises.

◆ Position two $\frac{3}{4}$-inch offset hinges on one of the doors, placing them about 3 inches from the top and bottom.

◆ For the hinge mortises, outline the edges and thickness of the hinge leaves on the door. Then cut around the outline with a chisel and mallet.

◆ With the chisel beveled side up, make a series of shallow cuts to shave the recess to the thickness of the hinge. Repeat to cut the second mortise (left).

◆ To fasten each hinge to the door, position the leaf in its mortise, mark the screw holes with an awl, and drive $\frac{3}{4}$-inch No. 8 wood screws.

4. Hanging the doors.

◆ With a helper holding one door in position against the cabinet, mark the edges and thickness of the portion of the hinge leaf on the front edge of the cabinet side. Cut a mortise at each outline—the leaves on the inside of the side panel sit flush on the surface. Fasten the hinge leaves to the cabinet (right).

◆ Install the other door the same way.

◆ Attach a magnetic catch assembly to the underside of the cabinet top and the inside top corners of the doors.

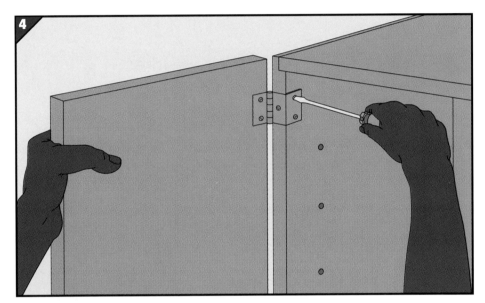

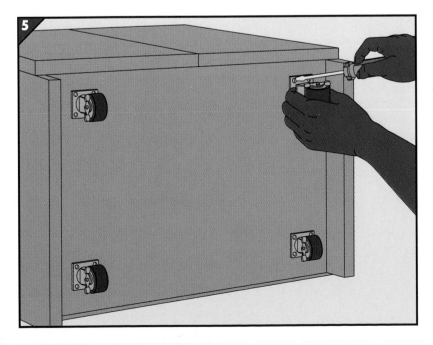

5. Adding casters and shelves.

◆ With the cabinet on its side, position a swivel-type locking caster on the bottom far enough from one corner so it will not bump against a cabinet side when it rotates. Fasten the caster in place with the screws provided, then install the remaining ones (left).

◆ Make shelves from $\frac{3}{4}$-inch plywood, cutting them $\frac{1}{8}$ inch shorter than the inside dimensions of the cabinet to allow for an easy fit. Insert shelf supports in the holes in the side panels and slide the shelves in position.

Hardware, lumber, and other workshop materials need to be stored in an organized fashion. The resulting lack of clutter will not only make your shop more efficient—the space will be safer.

Shelving: Mounted on L-shaped brackets, shelving can sit over a workbench or cover a wall (*below and opposite*). On interior partition walls without insulation, you can remove a section of wallboard and install narrow shelves between the studs (*page 116*). These shelves can be either stationary or, when held by metal standards and shelf supports, adjustable. Joist-supported shelves—ideal for masonry walls—are another option (*page 117*).

Storing Hardware: Small shop materials can be conveniently stored in containers of various sizes. These are easy to track and less apt to break or spill when anchored to shelves (*page 118*) or collected in drawers.

Drawers can be subdivided into small compartments or fitted with inserts to organize jars (*pages 118-119*). You can maximize the space in a deep drawer by installing a tray in the upper part (*page 120*).

Stacking Lumber: Store lumber on racks that keep it off the floor—out of the way but still accessible (*page 121*).

TOOLS

Electronic stud finder
Carpenter's level
Awl
Electric drill
Screwdriver
Tape measure
Circular saw
Combination square
Wallboard saw
Pry bar
Hammer
Plumb bob
Coping saw
Compass
C-clamp
Saber saw
Wrench
Woodworking vise

MATERIALS

Shelf brackets
1 x 2s, 1 x 4s, 1 x 6s
2 x 4s, 2 x 6s
Shims
Plywood ($\frac{1}{2}$", $\frac{3}{4}$")
Hardboard ($\frac{1}{8}$", $\frac{1}{4}$")
Common nails ($\frac{3}{4}$", 1", 1$\frac{1}{2}$", 2", 3", 3$\frac{1}{2}$")
Finishing nails (1$\frac{1}{2}$")
Masonry nails (3")
Wood screws ($\frac{3}{4}$", 1$\frac{1}{2}$", 2" No. 8)
Round-head wood screws ($\frac{5}{8}$" No. 6)
Lag screws ($\frac{3}{8}$" x 3", 4", 4$\frac{1}{2}$"), washers
Screw anchors
Construction adhesive
Shelf standards and clips
Wood glue

SAFETY TIPS

Wear goggles when nailing or when operating power tools.

WALL-MOUNTED SHELVES

1. Positioning and cutting the shelf.

◆ For a stud wall, locate and mark the proposed shelf height on every second stud. With a level, mark a vertical line on the center of the studs.
◆ Center a shelf bracket just below the height mark at one end of the desired shelf span. Center the bracket's vertical arm on the vertical line, then mark the screw holes with an awl (*right*).
◆ Drill a pilot hole for 1$\frac{1}{2}$-inch No. 8 wood screws at each awl mark, then fasten the bracket to the stud.
◆ Cut a shelf from $\frac{3}{4}$-inch plywood or 1-inch lumber, limiting its width so it will extend beyond the front arm of the bracket by no more than one-third the arm's length. Make the shelf long enough to stretch 4 to 6 inches past each end bracket.
◆ Position the shelf on the wall with one end on the installed bracket, and transfer the stud marks to the underside of the shelf; take the shelf down, and use a combination square to extend the lines across the shelf.

For a masonry wall, mark the proposed location of the shelf using a level. Cut the shelf to the desired length, but limit its width as described above.

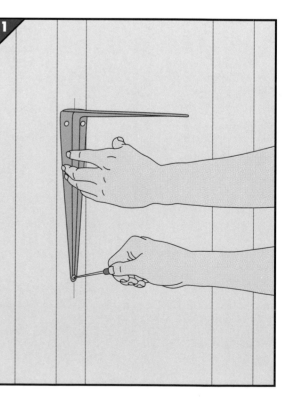

2. Fastening brackets to the shelf.

◆ Center a shelf bracket on one of the marked lines on the shelf, butting it against a combination square to position it flush with the edge of the shelf.
◆ Mark the screw-hole locations on the shelf *(above)*, drill a pilot hole for $\frac{3}{4}$-inch screws at each mark, and fasten the bracket to the shelf.
◆ Attach the remaining bracket in the same way.

For the masonry-wall shelf, space the brackets equally along the length of the shelf, then fasten them in place.

3. Fastening the shelf.

◆ Reposition the shelf on the installed bracket. With a helper, level the shelf, then mark the screw-hole locations for each bracket *(left)*.
◆ Remove the shelf, drill a pilot hole for $1\frac{1}{2}$-inch screws at each mark, then fasten the brackets to the studs.
◆ Screw the first bracket to the underside of the shelf.

On the masonry wall, position the shelf on the wall and mark the bracket holes. Drill a pilot hole at each mark, drive in masonry anchors, and secure the brackets.

STORAGE BETWEEN WALL STUDS

1. Backing the shelf area.
◆ Turn off the power to electrical circuits in the work area in case you cut into wires.
◆ With a wallboard saw, cut out a section of wallboard to expose the studs behind the wall. Remove any fire stops—boards fastened horizontally between studs—from the exposed area.
◆ To protect the wallboard on the other side of the wall, cut a $\frac{1}{4}$-inch hardboard panel to fit each gap between the exposed studs, spread construction adhesive on one side of the panel, and gently press it into place *(left)*.

SOLE PLATE

2. Marking shelf locations.
At each position for the first tier of shelves, hold a level across two adjoining studs and mark level lines on their front edges *(right)*.

SUPPORT

3. Mounting the shelves.
◆ Cut two 1-by-4 supports for each shelf, making them $\frac{3}{4}$ inch shorter than the distance from the sole plate to the shelf-location mark.
◆ Cut 1-by-6 or 1-by-4 shelves to fit between the studs.
◆ Set the shelf supports on the sole plate, flat against the insides of the studs, and nail them in place with 2-inch common nails.
◆ Lay each shelf on its supports and toenail two nails through each end into the stud *(left)*.
◆ Mount more tiers of shelves the same way, resting the supports on the first tier.

ANCHORING SHELVES TO JOISTS

1. Installing the frame.

◆ For joists perpendicular to the shelves, hang a plumb bob from the outside faces of the joists at each end of the proposed shelf and have a helper mark the floor where the bob touches it. Measure the distance between the marks and cut a pressure-treated 2-by-6 3 inches longer than this length. Position the board with each end extending $1\frac{1}{2}$ inches beyond each mark. Holding the baseboard against the wall, shim it level, if necessary, and fasten it to the floor with 3-inch masonry nails.

◆ For the end joists and every second joist in between, cut a 2-by-6 support to span from the baseboard to 6 inches above the bottom edge of the joists. Fasten the top of the supports to the joists with three 3-inch common nails *(left)*.

◆ Check each support for plumb with a level, then toenail the bottom to the baseboard with $3\frac{1}{2}$-inch nails.

For joists running parallel to the shelving, first cut 2-by-6 blocking to fit between the joist resting on the top plate and the next joist at 32-inch intervals. Fasten the blocking to the joists and

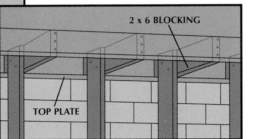

toenail it to the joist on the top plate with $3\frac{1}{2}$-inch nails. Then prepare the baseboard and supports, anchoring the supports to the blocking rather than the joists *(inset)*.

2. Installing shelf standards and shelving.

◆ Mark locations for metal shelf standards on the inside faces of the shelf supports $1\frac{1}{2}$ inches from the front and back edges at the top, middle, and bottom *(above)*. At each location, set a standard on the baseboard, align it with the trio of marks, and drill pilot holes for the screws provided. Then fasten the stan-

dard to the support. To prevent the screws on the other side of the same support from hitting each other, align the second standard on the opposite side of the location marks.

◆ Snap shelf clips into the standards *(inset)*, then cut the shelves from 1-by-6 lumber to fit between adjoining supports.

HANGING CONTAINERS

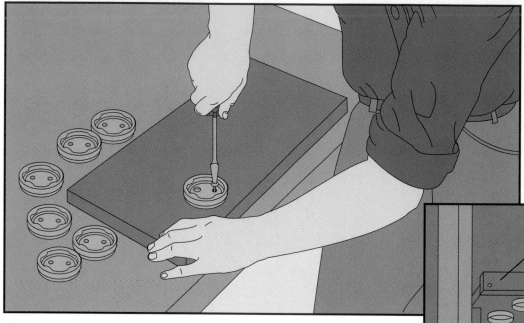

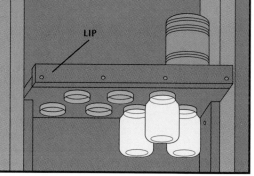

LIP

Fitting a shelf for storage.
◆ For every container to be hung, outline its lid on the underside of the shelf. Leave about 2 inches of clearance between outlines and stagger them so all the jars will be visible.
◆ With a nail, punch two holes through each lid for $\frac{5}{8}$-inch No. 6 round-head wood screws, then fasten the lids to the shelf *(above)*.
◆ To keep objects stored on the shelf top from slipping off, fasten a 1-by-2 lip to the front edge of the shelf with $1\frac{1}{2}$-inch finishing nails *(inset)*, then install the shelf and screw the jars into their lids.

EGG-CRATE COMPARTMENTS TO ORGANIZE A DRAWER

1. Cutting and marking divider strips.
◆ Determine the size and number of compartments you want in the drawer.
◆ Cut two sets of divider strips from $\frac{1}{8}$-inch hardboard—one set to fit lengthwise and one to fit widthwise in the drawer. Make them $\frac{1}{2}$ inch narrower than the height of the drawer.
◆ Draw a guideline $\frac{1}{4}$ inch off center down the length of one strip from each set, then use a combination square to mark compartment-intersection lines perpendicular to the guideline across the wider portion of the strip *(right)*.

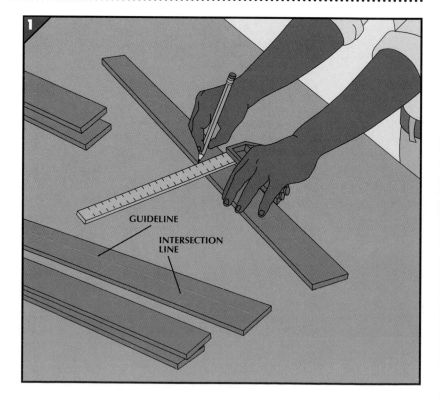

GUIDELINE

INTERSECTION LINE

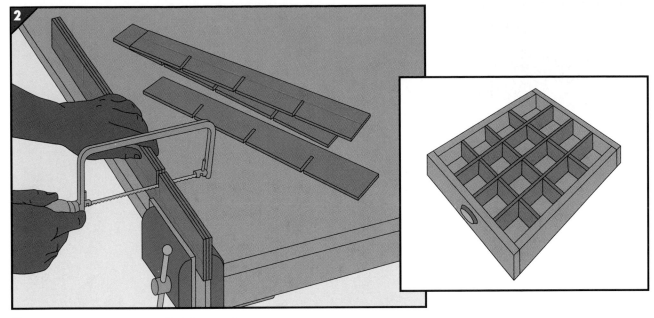

2. Cutting slots in the divider strips.

◆ Stack each set of divider strips with the marked strip on the outside, align the ends of the strips, then clamp one set on edge in a vise so the intersection lines face up. Cut along both sides of each line with a coping saw to make a slot $\frac{1}{8}$ inch wide, pushing out the waste wood at each slot *(above)*.

◆ Cut the other set in the same way.

◆ Assemble the strips by interlocking the lengthwise strips with the width-wise ones, aligning the slots. Place the assembly in the drawer *(inset)*.

A DIVIDER FOR JARS

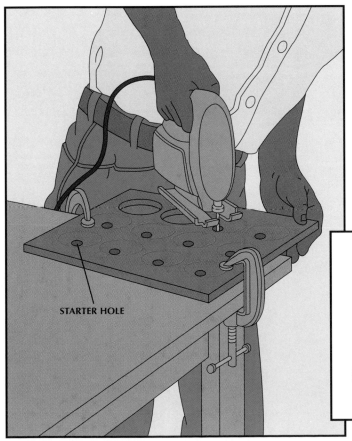

STARTER HOLE

Preparing the insert.

◆ Cut a piece of $\frac{1}{2}$-inch plywood to fit flat into the bottom of the drawer.

◆ On the plywood, outline the bottoms of the jars to be stored in the drawer, then use a compass to enlarge the radius of each circle by $\frac{1}{4}$ inch. Place a wood scrap under the divider and drill a $\frac{1}{2}$-inch starter hole for a saber-saw blade in each circle.

◆ Clamp the plywood over the edge of a worktable. Cut out the circles with a saber saw *(left)*.

◆ Slip the insert into the drawer and stand jars in the holes *(inset)*.

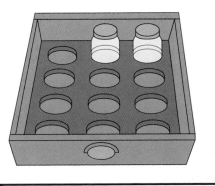

1. Assembling the tray.

◆ From a piece of $\frac{1}{2}$-inch plywood one-half as wide as the inside height of the drawer sides, cut two lengths $\frac{1}{8}$ inch shorter than the inside width of the drawer, and two more pieces one-half as long as the inside length of the sides.

◆ With wood glue and $1\frac{1}{2}$-inch common nails, assemble the pieces into a boxlike tray *(left)*.

◆ Cut a bottom from a piece of $\frac{1}{8}$-inch hardboard and fasten it to the tray with wood glue and 1-inch nails.

◆ Make egg-crate dividers for the tray if desired *(pages 118-119)*.

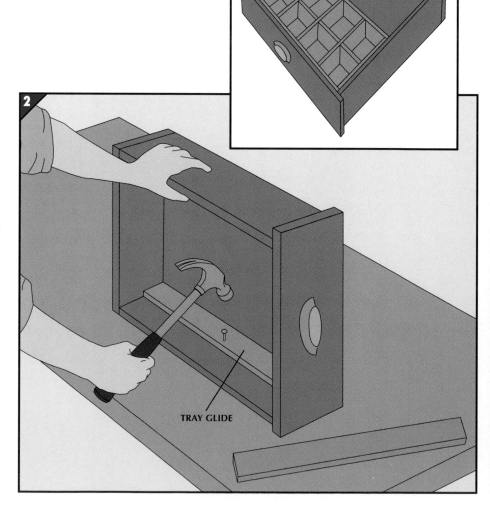

TRAY GLIDE

2. Installing the glides.

◆ For each glide, cut a piece of $\frac{1}{2}$-inch plywood one-half as wide as the inside height of the drawer sides and equal to their inside length.

◆ Set a glide in the drawer flat against the inside of one drawer side. Fasten it with glue and $\frac{3}{4}$-inch common nails *(right)*. Install the other glide to the opposite side.

Slide the tray back and forth on the glides, as needed, to access the items in the drawer *(inset)*.

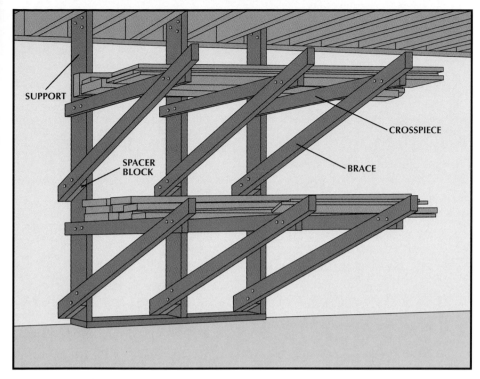

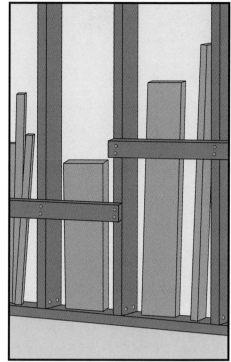

A lumber rack for a masonry wall.

The framework of the rack illustrated above can be built as on page 117 with $\frac{3}{8}$- by 3-inch lag screws and washers used to fasten the supports to the joists. The crosspieces on which the lumber will sit are 2-by-4s cut to 3-foot lengths; to 4-inch lengths for the spacer blocks; and to $5\frac{1}{2}$-foot lengths for the braces. One end of each brace is mitered at a 45-degree angle. The crosspieces and supports and the braces and crosspieces are joined by two lag screws at each connection. For the brace-support connections, two $4\frac{1}{2}$-inch lag screws are used with a spacer block in between. For a wall with exposed studs, you can forgo the supports and fasten the braces and crosspieces directly to the studs.

Making use of exposed studs.

Dowels, moldings, and other small lumber pieces can be stored by nailing wood strips across the front of the studs *(above)*.

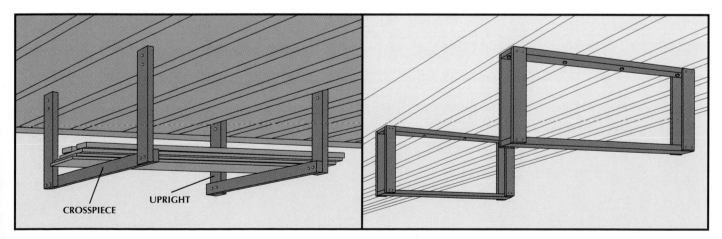

Storing lumber overhead.

For a shop with exposed ceiling joists, four 30-inch-long 2-by-4s are cut for uprights and two 4-foot lengths are cut for the crosspieces. The uprights are attached to the joists and the crosspieces to the uprights with $\frac{3}{8}$- by 3-inch lag screws and washers; the uprights on the same joist are spaced 4 feet apart and the second pair is positioned about 6 feet away from the first *(above, left)*.

For a finished ceiling, four $49\frac{1}{2}$-inch-long crosspieces are cut from 2-by-4 stock and eight 24-inch uprights are cut from 1-by-4 stock. The two frames are built by joining the uprights to the crosspieces with wood glue and 2-inch No. 8 wood screws. The frames are fastened to the center of four of the joists about 6 feet apart with 4-inch lag screws *(above, right)*.

Power tools produce a tremendous amount of dust. In addition to the mess this creates, long-term exposure to airborne particles can lead to chronic respiratory problems.

You can protect your lungs by wearing a dust mask or respirator. A more thorough solution is a system that collects dust at the source. This system combined with good ventilation or an air-filtration box *(pages 17-18)* can remove virtually all wood dust from shop air.

Portable Dust Collection: Shop vacuums and portable dust collectors can be wheeled around and hooked up to any tool. Vacuums offer the most economical solution. Powered by universal-type motors, they have good suction capacity; however, they cannot move huge volumes of air or manage large wood chips such as those from a planer or jointer. Portable dust collectors *(below)* are designed to handle much more waste than shop vacuums.

With either machine, you need a means of directing dust from the tool to the collector. The simplest solution is to attach a vacuum hose to the tool with an adapter or a shop-made dust hood *(opposite)*.

A Central System: Instead of removing the dust at each tool, you can assemble a system in which all the shop tools are connected with ducting or polyvinylchloride (PVC) pipe to one stationary dust collector *(pages 124-125)*, or to a large portable model. A dealer can help you choose the best machine for your shop. If you use PVC, ground it to prevent the buildup of static electricity *(page 124, Step 2)*, which can ignite wood dust.

 TOOLS

Screwdriver	Hacksaw
Hammer	Coping saw
Tin snips	Electric drill
	Caulking gun
	Dust collector

 **MATERIALS**

Hose clamps	Jumper wire
PVC pipe, Ys,	Stranded copper
reducers, sweeps,	wire (14-gauge)
caps, and elbows	Wire caps
(3" or larger)	Duct tape
Perforated metal	Silicone caulk
strapping	Flexible hose (3")
Roofing nails ($1\frac{1}{2}$")	Reducers and
Hardboard ($\frac{1}{8}$")	adapters
	Wet/dry vacuum
	hose and head

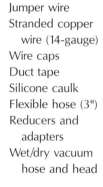 **SAFETY TIPS**

Wear goggles when nailing or when using power tools. Put on heavy-duty gloves when handling sheet metal.

The workings of a dust collector.
Portable dust collectors can be wheeled to any tool in the shop or hooked up to a modest central system *(page 124)*. A machine rated to move at least 500 cubic feet of air per minute is adequate for most home workshops.

The machine shown here is a two-stage collector. Debris- and dust-laden air is drawn in below the motor so most of the heavier particles drop into the waste container. The finer dust passes through the blower and into the filter bag. Filtered air is exhausted from the machine.

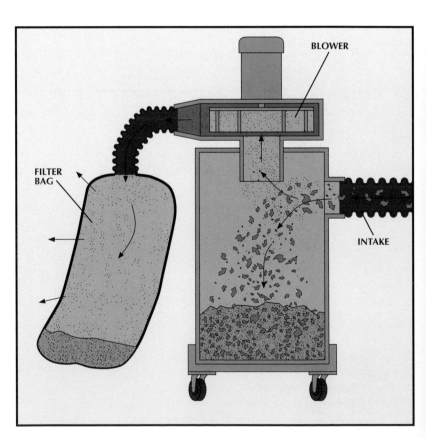

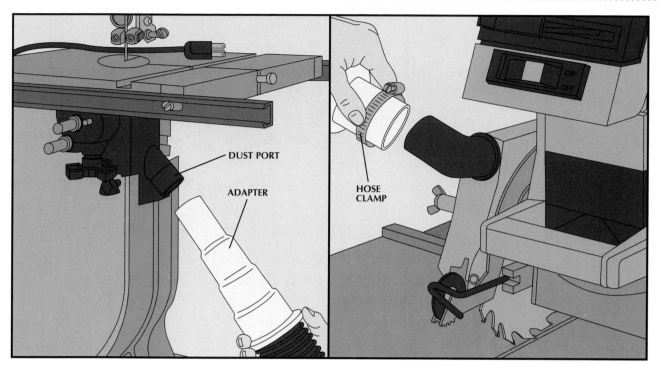

DUST PORT

ADAPTER

HOSE CLAMP

Connecting to a dust port.

Choose an adapter for the dust-collector or shop vacuum hose that connects to the tool's dust port snugly with a friction fit *(above, left)*. If the part of the tool with the dust port moves, such as the motor of a radial-arm saw, reinforce the adapter with a hose clamp *(above, right)*.

TRICKS OF THE TRADE

Shop-Made Metal Dust Hoods

To make a dust hood for almost any machine, you can modify a sheet-metal boot for heating ducts. With rivets or sheet-metal screws, fasten on extra flanges *(left)* so the hood fits snugly around the opening on the tool where wood chips and dust are expelled. You can also fashion an open-ended box from pieces of galvanized sheet metal with tabs that can be folded over and fastened to the adjoining piece; the example shown at right will capture most of the dust generated by a planer. Whichever design you choose, experiment with cardboard and duct tape to find the right fit, then cut the sheet metal with tin snips and attach the pieces together. Fasten it to the tool with stove bolts, duct tape, or sheet-metal screws; and attach the flexible hose to it with a hose clamp.

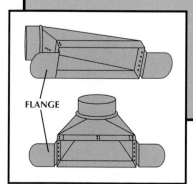

FLANGE

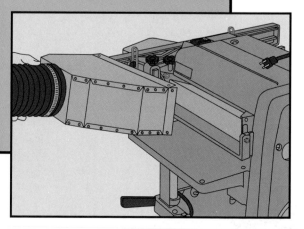

INSTALLING A CENTRAL SYSTEM

Layout of the system.

In this workshop, 3-inch PVC pipe—connected to a dust collector at one end and capped at the other—runs along the wall above stationary tools and the workbench. The pipes are suspended from ceiling joists with hanger straps *(Step 1, below).* Sweeps that turn corners in a radius of 24 inches or more are less likely to get clogged than standard pipe elbows. Ys branch to flexible hoses running to the machines and to a vacuum attachment at the bench. A short length of pipe attached to each Y contains a blast gate, either commercial or shop-made *(Step 2, below),* used to cut a tool off from the system when the tool is not operating.

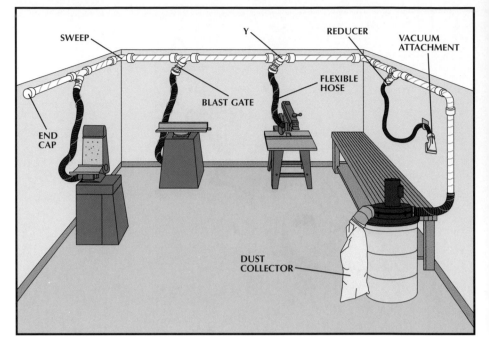

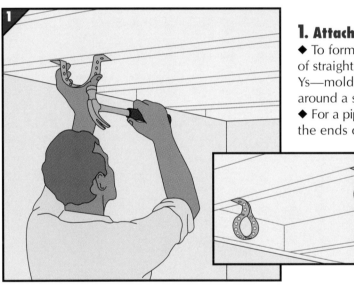

1. Attaching the hanger straps.

◆ To form hangers—you'll need one for every 4-foot run of straight pipe and another for each side of all elbows and Ys—mold 12-inch lengths of perforated metal strapping around a section of 3-inch PVC pipe.

◆ For a pipe running perpendicular to ceiling joists, bend out the ends of the hangers to form flanges. Nail through the flanges into a joist with $1\frac{1}{2}$-inch roofing nails *(left).* For a pipe running parallel to a joist under a finished ceiling, bend the ends of the hanger so they overlap and nail it to a joist through both ends at once *(inset).* For an unfinished ceiling, nail the straps to the sides of the joist.

2. Making blast gates.

Commercial devices are available, but you can also fashion inexpensive blast gates.

◆ For each gate, saw a $\frac{1}{8}$-inch kerf halfway through a short section of 3-inch PVC pipe.

◆ Cut a gate from $\frac{1}{8}$-inch hardboard to fit in the kerf, then saw a semicircle in one half of the gate the same size as the inside diameter of the pipe; leave the other half intact so that it can protrude from the kerf to form a handle.

◆ To seal the slot when the machine is in use and the blast gate is removed, cut a sleeve from the same size pipe with a diagonal slit to allow it to fit around the pipe and slide over the kerf.

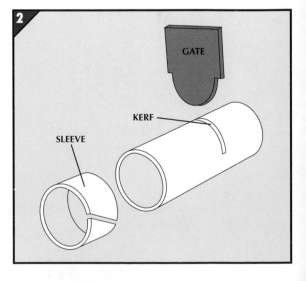

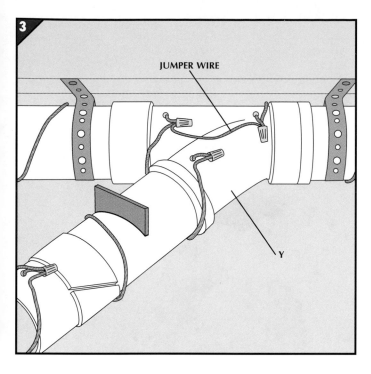

JUMPER WIRE

Y

3. Joining and grounding pipe sections.
◆ Drill a $\frac{1}{8}$-inch hole through both ends of each Y.
◆ Run 14-gauge stranded copper wire through a length of pipe, then slide the pipe through the hanging straps.
◆ Thread the wire through the drilled hole in the Y, then fit the Y onto the pipe. Do not use PVC glue, but if any Ys are loose, secure them with duct tape.
◆ Wrap another wire around the outside of the pipe.
◆ Twist together the inner and outer wires with jumper wires to join the first length of pipe to the Y, and fasten them with a wire cap. Seal the hole with a dab of caulk.
◆ Continue adding pipe and connectors, grounding each elbow in the same way.
◆ Ground each blast gate but, instead of a jumper wire, add a wire long enough to reach the tool; then insert the blast gates in the Ys *(left)*.

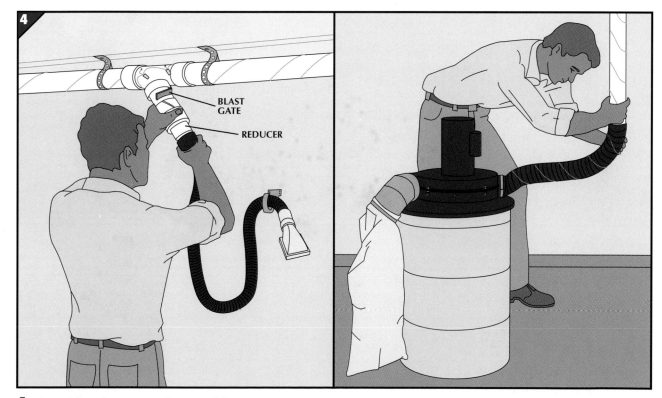

BLAST GATE

REDUCER

4. Attaching hoses to the machines.
◆ With 3-inch flexible hose, connect the vertical branches to the tools *(page 123)*, adding adapters and reducers as necessary. The flexible hose does not require grounding, but wrap the long wire around it, and attach the wire to the grounding screw on the tool's motor or switch.
◆ To make the vacuum attachment, buy a hose and vacuum head for a wet/dry vacuum and fit them together. Fasten a hook to the wall to hang the hose. Plug a reducer into a vertical branch, then fit the hose cuff around the reducer *(above, left)*.
◆ Hook up the dust collector to the end of the run of pipe with 3-inch flexible hose *(above, right)*; secure the hose with a hose clamp. Attach the ground wire from the main run of pipe to the grounding screw on the switch or motor of the collector.
◆ At the far end of the run, close off the end of the main line with an end cap.

INDEX

A

Air quality: air-filtration boxes, 17; exhaust fans, 17-18, 100-102
Armored cable: 61
Asbestos safety: 17
Attic workshops: 8
Awls: 28

B

Band saws: 34; in confined spaces, 45; roller stands, 86
Basements: moisture problems, 12-13; workshop locations, 8
Belt sanders: 27, 29; belt-sander catapult , 42
Bench dogs: 67
Bench grinders: 38
Bits: drill-press bits, 35; router bits, 108, 110
Blades: scroll-saw blades, 34; table-saw blades, 31
Borers: multipurpose power tool, 38
Brick sets: 26, 28

C

Cabinets on wheels: 111-113
Carpentry tools: 26-29
Carrying tools: 94-95
Ceilings, soundproofing: 22, 23
Chalk lines: 28
Chemical safety: 10
Childproofing power tools: 11, 61
Chisels: 26, 28, 37
Circuit breakers: GFCIs, 53, 56; 120-volt breakers, 53; 240-volt breakers, 57
Circuits. *See* Wiring
Circular saws: 27, 29
Clamps: 26, 28
Combination squares: 28
Concrete walls, repairing: 13
Condensation on cold-water pipes: 12
Conduit: 54-56

D

Dadoes, cutting: 108
Dollies: 47
Doors: pass-through slots, 19-

20; soundproofing, 22, 23
Drawers: 108-110; egg-crate compartments, 118-119; jar dividers, 119; sliding trays, 120
Drill presses: 35; multipurpose power tool, 38, 39; safety, 41; tilting tables, 91
Drills, electric: 27, 29; manual, 26; star drills, 29
Ducts, soundproofing: 23
Dust collectors: 122; blast gates, 124; connecting to tools, 123; grounding PVC pipes, 124; installing central systems, 124-125; metal dust hoods, 123

E

Electrical safety: 10, 11, 40, 54, 61
Electrical systems. *See* Wiring
Electric baseboard heaters: 14, 16; circuits required, 48
Electric-cord covers: 59. *See also* Raceways
Electric tools: 26-29
Exhaust fans: 17-18; in spray booths, 100-102
Extension-cord reels: 59
Extension tables: 33, 82, 83-85

F

Fans: 17-18; in spray booths, 100-102
Featherboards: 40, 43, 90
File cards: 26, 29
Files: 26, 28
Filters: 17
Fire extinguishers: 10
Fire safety: 10
Floor plans, workshop: 44-47
Floors, soundproofing: 22
Fluorescent fixtures, wiring: 62-66
Foundations: repairing cracks, 13; water problems, 12-13
Furnace ducts: 14-15

G

Garage workshops: 8, 46
GFCIs (ground-fault circuit interrupters): 48, 49, 53, 56
Grinders: 38

H

Hammers: 27, 28
Handsaws: 26, 28
Hanger bolts: 91
Hangers: 106, 107
Hanging jars: 118
Hearing protection: 21
Heating: cabinets in unheated workshops, 16; circuits required for electric baseboard heaters, 48; electric baseboard heaters, 14, 16; forced-air furnace ducts, 14-15
Honing guides: 27
Humidity, testing for: 12
Hygrometers: 12

J

Jar storage: 118, 119
Jigs: featherboards, 40, 43, 90; miter jigs, 88; mortising jigs, 89; push sticks, 90; tablesaw crosscut jigs, 87-88; tapering jigs, 89; tenoning jigs, 89; tilting drill-press tables, 91
Jointers: 36; in confined spaces, 45; multipurpose power tool, 38; safety, 43, 90

L

Lamps. *See* Lighting
Lathes: 37; lathe-tool flipping, 42; multipurpose power tool, 38, 39; tools, 37
Layouts, workshop: 44-47
Lazy Susans: 103
Lead safety: 17
Levels: 27, 28
Lighting: 67; wiring fluorescent fixtures, 62-66. *See also* Wiring
Locations for workshops: 8-9, 46-47
Locking power tools: 11, 61
Lumber racks: 121

M

Maintenance tools: 26-29
Marking gauges: 27, 29
Masonry tools: 26-29
Measuring tools: 27, 28, 29

H (second column)

Metalworking benches: 98-99
Metalworking vises: 76, 99
Miter boxes: 26, 28
Miter jigs: 88
Moisture problems. *See* Water problems
Mortises, chiseling: 113
Mortising jigs: 89
Multipurpose power tools: 38-39

N

Nail sets: 29
Noise reduction. *See* Soundproofing

O

Outlets. *See* Receptacles

P

Painting booths: 100-102
Pass-through slots: 19-20
Pegboard: 106, 107
Pipe cutters: 28
Planers, electric: 36
Planes: 27, 29
Planing attachments for saws: 32
Pliers: 27, 29
Plugs, locking: 11
Plumbing tools: 26-29
Plungers: 29
Portable power tools. *See* Power tools, portable
Power bars: 58
Power-cord covers: 59. *See also* Raceways
Power tools, portable: 27, 29; disabling, 11, 61
Power-tool safety: belt-sander catapult, 42; disabling power tools, 11, 61; drill-press twirl, 41; flanged switches, 61; jointer jump, 43; lathe-tool flipping, 42; radial-arm saw kickback, 41; router-table hazards, 43; table-saw kickback, 40
Power tools for confined spaces: 38-39, 45
Power tools, stationary: 30-39; band saws, 34; bench grinders, 38; circuits required, 48; disabling, 11, 61; drill presses, 35;

TIME-LIFE® BOOKS

Time-Life Books is a division of Time Life Inc.

TIME LIFE INC.
PRESIDENT and CEO: George Artandi

TIME-LIFE BOOKS
PRESIDENT: John D. Hall
PUBLISHER/MANAGING EDITOR:
Neil Kagan

HOME REPAIR AND IMPROVEMENT:
The Home Workshop
EDITOR: Lee Hassig
MARKETING DIRECTOR: James Gillespie
Art Director: Kathleen Mallow
Associate Editor/Research and Writing:
Karen Sweet
Marketing Manager: Wells Spence

Vice President, Director of Finance:
Christopher Hearing
Vice President, Book Production:
Marjann Caldwell
Director of Operations: Eileen Bradley
Director of Photography and Research:
John Conrad Weiser
Director of Editorial Administration:
Barbara Levitt (Acting)
Production Manager: Marlene Zack
Quality Assurance Manager: James King
Library: Louise D. Forstall

ST. REMY MULTIMEDIA INC.
President and Chief Executive Officer:
Fernand Lecoq
President and Chief Operating Officer:
Pierre Léveillé
Vice President, Finance: Natalie Watanabe
Managing Editor: Carolyn Jackson
Managing Art Director: Diane Denoncourt
Production Manager: Michelle Turbide

Staff for The Home Workshop

Series Editors: Marc Cassini, Heather Mills
Series Art Director: Francine Lemieux
Art Director: Robert Paquet
Assistant Editor: John Dowling
Designers: Jean-Guy Doiron, Robert Labelle
Editorial Assistant: James Piecowye
Coordinator: Dominique Gagné
Copy Editor: Judy Yelon
Indexer: Linda Cardella Cournoyer
Systems Coordinator: Éric Beaulieu
Other Staff: Linda Castle, Lorraine Doré

PICTURE CREDITS
Cover: Photograph, Robert Chartier.
Art, Robert Paquet.

Illustrators: Jack Arthur, Terry Atkinson, Gilles Beauchemin, Frederic F. Bigio (B-C Graphics), Laszlo Bodrogi, François Daxhelet, Roger Essley, Charles Forsythe, Forte Inc., Gerry Gallagher, William J. Hennessy Jr. (A and W Graphics), Elsie Hennig, Walter Hilmers Jr. (HJ Commercial Art), Dick Lee, John Martinez, John Massey, Joan S. McGurren, Jacques Perrault, Eduino J. Pereira, Melissa B. Pooré, Ray Skibinski, Snowden Associates. Inc.

Photographers: **End papers:** Glenn Moores and Chantal Lamarre. **10:** (left) First Alert Inc.; (right) Robert Chartier. **12, 31, 32, 34, 35, 37, 38, 58, 90, 91, 99, 108:** Robert Chartier. **36:** Delta International Machinery Corp. **89:** (upper) Woodcraft Supply Corp.; (lower) Delta International Machinery Corp. **110:** Glenn Moores and Chantal Lamarre

ACKNOWLEDGMENTS
The editors wish to thank the following individuals and institutions: CMT Tools Inc., Oldsmar, FL; Delta International Machinery Corp., Guelph, Ont.; First Alert Inc., Aurora, IL; General Cable Corp., Highland Heights, KY; Hitachi Power Tools U.S.A. Ltd., Norcross, GA; Norton Canada Inc., Hamilton, Ont.; Record Tools Inc., Pickering, Ont.; Stanley Hardware, Division of Stanley Canada Inc., Oakville, Ont.; ToolTrend Ltd., Concord, Ont.; Wilke Machinery Co., Inc., York, PA; Woodcraft Supply Corp., Parkersburg, WV; Woodstock International Inc., Bellingham, WA

Library of Congress
Cataloging-in-Publication Data
The home workshop / by the editors of
 Time-Life Books.
 p. cm. — (Home repair and improvement)
Includes index.
ISBN 0-7835-3909-6
1. Workshops—Design and construction.
 2. Workshops—Equipment and supplies.
 3. Woodworking tools.
I. Time-Life Books. II. Series.
TT152.H6 1997
648'.08—dc21   97-4083